Praise for

Tomorrow's Change Makers

"Marilyn's research study, based on interviews with highly engaged youth, is a scholarly, insightful, and impressive contribution to the field of civic engagement."

—**Peter Levine, PhD**, Associate Dean for Research, Tufts University
Jonathan M. Tisch College of Citizenship and Public Service

"This deeply researched, thought-provoking book shows insightful glimpses into the lives of children who grew up to care about the world and make it a more just and compassionate place in which to live. The stories are not only instructive for educators, civic leaders, and policy makers, they also show parents that developing core abilities in children helps them grow into young adults who are capable of charting their own moral lives of meaning and purpose."

—**Michele Borba, EdD**, author of *Building Moral Intelligence*

"Marilyn's research and thinking inspires us to dive more deeply into the important work of engaging youth in our communities."

—**Amy Smith**, President, generationOn, a POINTS OF LIGHT
organization that mobilizes youth to change the world through service

"*Tomorrow's Change Makers* investigates the dynamic relationship between two essential elements of becoming a person—personal identity and worldview. Through the voices of her participants, Dr. Price-Mitchell reminds us how young people discover motivation and passion to improve the lives of others. This is inspiring and useful research for those who work with youth."

—**Stephen D. Arnold, PhD**, Co-founder and Vice Chairman
GEORGE LUCAS EDUCATIONAL FOUNDATION

"Guided by Dr. Price-Mitchell's profound wisdom and groundbreaking research, *Tomorrow's Change Makers* gives parents, educators, and community leaders the tools to cultivate and inspire positive youth development. By giving the next generation opportunities to develop empathy and empowering them to make a difference, we can reduce prejudice, inequality, racism, and bullying. This book is a must-read for anyone who loves a child and wants to see a better world."

—**Rachel Macy Stafford**, New York Times bestselling author
of *Hands Free Mama* & *Hands Free Life*

"For those who are worried about our kids and our country, *Tomorrow's Change Makers* offers inspiration and hope. Best of all, it is chock full of insights and action steps that can help change the lives of young people you may work with, know, or love."

—**Marguerite Kondracke**, retired CEO,
AMERICA'S PROMISE ALLIANCE

Dr. Price-Mitchell's research will be of interest to every teacher, parent, and counselor who hopes to inspire citizenship and positive development in young people."

—**Judith Stevens-Long, PhD**, Malcolm Knowles Professor
of Adult Learning, FIELDING GRADUATE UNIVERSITY

"Democracy is a gift that requires the development of social consciousness and community engagement from early childhood onward. Young people want to belong to something greater than themselves and to feel significant. When they are not taught to fulfill these desires in useful ways, they are likely to find useless ways to fill the void. This book provides tools and skills to help kids improve their own lives and the world around them. It is a must-read for anyone interested in nurturing the positive growth of today's children."

—**Jane Nelsen, EdD,** author of the *Positive Discipline Series*

"Preparing our youngest citizens to become engaged in civic life is an essential task for families, schools, and communities, one that requires thoughtful and serious investment. This well-researched, insightful book shows how young people develop the passion to improve society, and how supportive adults can guide them. An essential and pleasurable read for all who care about the future of democracy."

—**Anne T. Henderson**, author of *Beyond the Bake Sale*
Senior Consultant, ANNENBERG INSTITUTE FOR SCHOOL REFORM

"*Tomorrow's Change Makers* is one of the most important books I've read on the power of citizenship and the need to nurture new generations of citizens. It not only challenges current approaches to youth volunteerism and college resume-building, but also shows us how we can help young people become part of an engaged citizenry by way of their own heroic journeys in the world."

—**Jeff Leinaweaver, PhD**, author of *Storytelling for Sustainability*

TOMORROW'S
CHANGE
MAKERS

RECLAIMING THE POWER OF CITIZENSHIP
FOR A NEW GENERATION

MARILYN PRICE-MITCHELL, PhD

Publishing

FIRST EDITION

Publisher's Cataloging-in-Publication
Price-Mitchell, Marilyn, author.
   Tomorrow's change makers : reclaiming the power of citizenship for a new generation / Marilyn Price-Mitchell, PhD. -- First edition.
   pages cm
   Includes bibliographical references and index.
   LCCN 2015913497
   ISBN 978-0-9965851-0-1 (pbk.)
   ISBN 978-0-9965851-2-5 (eBook)
   1. Youth--Political activity--United States. 2. Political participation--United States. 3. Social participation--United States. 4. Democracy--United States. 5. Youth development--United States. I. Title.
   HQ799.2.P6P75 2015   305.2350973
                      QBI15-600173

Cover Design by DamonZa
Cover Photograph by Oledjio/Shutterstock.com
Indexing by Molly Hall

The Compass Advantage™ is a trademark owned by the author, Marilyn Price-Mitchell.

Names of research participants and the adults they described in their interviews have been changed to protect their identities.

To the memory of Richard E. Price, PhD,
who inspired me to be a lifelong learner

and

To our grandchildren, Lucy, Bryn, and Cooper,
whose treasured young lives inspire me each day.

Contents

Preface

A child of the 60's, I readily recall memories of civil unrest, protest marches, and committed citizen actions that changed the course of U.S. history. Yet during adolescence, my White middle-class family, school, and community failed in their responsibility to help me understand the critical civic and political issues of the day. Growing up, I never knew an African American because Black people did not live or attend school in my small suburb outside Detroit. Admittedly, even as a high school student, I did not think to ask why.

I knew that poor people lived in "slums," but my father taught me it was people's lack of hard work that landed them there. My parents were the pillars of our community, taking on important jobs like PTA president, church elder, Girl Scout troop leader, and school board member. While they volunteered their time generously, they did so within the borders of their own town where no one was Black, poor, or marginalized. They lived the American dream, full of hope for their children and a blessed ignorance of the world around them.

Like many of my generation, I was instilled with moral values, like honesty, compassion, and integrity. Yet I lived in social and political isolation until I started college in 1967. It was then that I experienced ethnic and religious diversity for the first time, hearing stories and ways of thinking distinct from my own. And although the stories were different, somehow a collective human story bridged our differences. We became engaged together to change the world.

Determined to make a difference, I protested the Vietnam War, volunteered in riot-ravaged areas of Detroit, and circulated petitions for a variety of civic causes. I sang and played guitar in coffee houses, often writing my own songs of peace and protest. Each experience pushed the boundaries of my young adulthood, enabling me to form an identity separate from my parents. I learned to think strategically, articulate goals, make plans, and organize others toward a common purpose. Linking actions to outcomes, I not only believed I was part of a special generation of young people, but I also constructed my identity as an American citizen.

While protests, petitions, and collective volunteer experiences propelled my energy for civic engagement in the late 1960s, a middle-aged African American woman would also play a role in my personal story. Patsy Chandler, a community activist and board member of the Red Cross, lived in a poor neighborhood on the outskirts of Ann Arbor. Her children grew up in a crime-infested neighborhood and her son served time in prison. Despite tremendous personal challenges, she devoted unending hours to community service.

Every March 13th, Patsy invited friends and civic leaders to celebrate her birthday. While they sipped tea and ate cake, she outlined her new annual cause and invited guests to contribute funds toward accomplishing her goal. During my tenure as a University of Michigan student intern at the Red Cross, Patsy Chandler announced that her 1970 Annual Tea would raise money to send me to the Red Cross National Convention as one of its first youth representatives. In doing so, she proclaimed her deep belief in the importance of youth development and civic engagement.

I was humbled by Patsy Chandler's action. While I mingled at the tea with Patsy's family and African American friends, I was struck by their authentic spirit, laughter, and sense of civic purpose. Yet I could not understand why a poor Black woman chose to bestow on me, a White middle-class kid from the suburbs, such an honor. Why not give money to a young Black student or to a more deserving social cause? Her answer was simple and straightforward: "Because I believe in your potential to serve youth, not just in your current position, but for a lifetime."

Patsy's insights would prove remarkably on target. Much of my career has been devoted to serving young people and to their healthy development as individuals. I often wondered what Patsy saw in me that I had yet to learn about myself. Was there a part of my young life story that predicted I would sustain a commitment to civic involvement? Were there challenges and obstacles I faced that helped me develop the initiative to make a difference? These and many other questions prompted my research about youth civic engagement and about the sustained initiative required by young people who are motivated by the principles of democracy and purposes greater than themselves.

Marilyn Price-Mitchell, PhD

Challenging the Status Quo

Strong, just, robust democracies require the skillful and committed participation of their citizens. It is easiest for people to obtain the necessary skills and commitments when they are young. Therefore, civic education—which is not just the name of a course, but is the shared responsibility of schools, families, political institutions, the press, and communities—is a critical component of a struggle to sustaining democracy itself.

— Peter Levine, PhD, *The Future of Democracy:*
Developing the Next Generation of American Citizens

When Jay Leno hosted *The Tonight Show*, he regularly took to the streets of Los Angeles to interview random people in a segment called *Jaywalking*. Often armed with fourth grade civics questions, his television audience roared with laughter at how young people responded.

"Who was the first President of the United States?" Leno asked one young man. "Benjamin. (pause) Benjamin Franklin!" he replied with certainty.

"What was the Gettysburg Address? Have you heard of it?" asked Leno of a young woman. She responded, "Sure, I've heard of it! But I don't know the exact address."

I recently had the opportunity to watch several recorded *Jaywalking* segments in the presence of retired U.S. Supreme Court Justice Sandra Day O'Connor. Indicating she had never seen Leno's street interviews before, O'Connor said, "Those aren't for real, are they?"

When someone in the room whispered, "Yes," I could feel the depth of her dismay.

"Oh my," O'Connor replied, "this is so very sad."

As it turns out, it is even sadder than what Justice O'Connor might have imagined.

OUR KIDS ARE FAILING DEMOCRACY 101

American youth not only earn failing grades when it comes to civics knowledge, but also show significant declines in civic engagement activities over the past several decades. In a study conducted by Coley and Sum (2012), the following were among the dismal findings:

- Only 25% of middle and high school students score at or about "proficient" in their knowledge of civics and American history.

- There is an unprecedented gap in the income and educational levels of those who vote and those who don't. The oldest, most highly educated, and highest income Americans are seven times more likely to vote than the youngest, least educated, and lowest income Americans.

- Volunteering, a driving force in American social change, is closely associated with age, educational attainment, and income. Young, poorly educated youth are highly disengaged from their communities.

While this research should beckon a call to action for American educational institutions, civic organizations, and families, it is not the first study or national survey to discover a declining lack of civics knowledge and engagement among younger U.S. citizens.

In 2011, a *New York Times* article pointed out the gloomy state of civics education in the U.S., including a study that found 75% of high school seniors could not name a power granted to Congress by the Constitution (Dillon, 2011). In response to the study's bleak findings, Justice O'Connor admonished, "We cannot afford to continue to neglect the preparation of future generations for active and informed citizenship."

In studies by the Center for Information and Research on Civic Learning and Engagement (CIRCLE), the decline in civic engagement and civic knowledge has been linked to all income and educational levels. In surveys of college freshman, a steep decline in political interests was found from 1966 to 2002. More recently, there was a 31 percent drop in the numbers of 18-29-year-olds who followed current news and affairs.

The results of these studies are decidedly worrisome. Our nation's less-educated, lower-income, and young adults have become disenfranchised from the voting and civic engagement process. Some will argue that their disenfranchisement is voluntary, and hold them responsible. But it's not that simple. When our schools are failing at educating a whole generation of citizens, the blame must be shared by everyone. As Levine (2007) said, the responsibility rests in "schools, families, political institutions, the press, and communities."

In 1954, Robert Maynard Hutchins, the head of the Ford Foundation and editor of *The Great Books,* said it best, "The death of democracy is not likely to be an assassination from ambush. It will be a slow extinction from apathy, indifference, and undernourishment."

The research is exceedingly clear. The days of civic apathy, indifference, and undernourishment are upon us. Democracy flourishes only when all people—rich and poor, young and old, skilled and unskilled—have a voice at the table of public discourse. When power is in the hands of a few, minority populations become oppressed and disenfranchised. Justice is not served. Freedom dwindles away. How many more studies do we need to understand that the future of democracy is at risk?

William Damon, one of the world's leading scholars of human development and Director of the Stanford University Center on Adolescence, sounds a grave alarm:

> The most serious danger Americans now face—greater than terrorism—is that our country's future may not end up in the hands of a citizenry capable of sustaining the liberty that has been America's most precious legacy. If trends continue, many young Americans will grow up without an understanding of the benefits, privileges, and duties of citizens in a free society, and without acquiring the habits of character needed to live responsibly in one (Damon, 2011).

BUILDING BLOCKS OF SOCIAL CHANGE

Unlike school-age children of past generations, today's young people are part of a diverse, global, and inter-connected knowledge society where opportunities for civic learning and engagement abound. Seventy-five percent of American high school students report their schools offer community service, and 21% say volunteer work is required (Zukin, Keeter, Andolina, Jenkins, & Carpini, 2006). Despite the fact that adolescents volunteer in their communities in higher numbers than ever (Levine, 2007, p. 84), almost two-thirds of young Americans today are considered disengaged (Lopez et al., 2006).

In fact, Putnam (2000) documents a 30-year declining trend in political and civic engagement in America, attributing the decline to an erosion of the quality of our personal and public lives. In a study of youth purpose, Damon (2008) confirmed political and societal interests to be one of the lowest ranking sources of purpose among today's teenagers.

Scholars agree that engagement in civic and political activities outside of school is an important building block of social change (Larson & Hansen, 2005). Some posit that direct participation in these types of activities helps young people internalize the practice of civic action (Youniss, McLellan, & Yates, 1997).

In *The Future of Democracy: Developing the Next Generation of American Citizens,* Levine (2007) argued that young people succeeded better in life when they were engaged in their communities. This assertion supports the literature that correlates positive developmental outcomes to meaningful community service, including the development of moral character, purpose, identity, and initiative (Damon, 2008; Larson, 2000; Larson & Hansen, 2005; Youniss & Yates, 1999).

Service experiences are linked to the development of social responsibility, less use of drugs and alcohol, and doing better in school (Zaff & Michelsen, 2002). Studies support the claim that these activities facilitate the development of compassion (Yates & Youniss, 1996), a greater understanding of democracy (Flanagan, Gallay, Gill, Gallay, & Nti, 2005), and moral identity that leads to greater community engagement in adulthood (Youniss, 2006). Longitudinal studies demonstrate that service learning in high school correlates with greater civic and community involvement in adulthood as many as 30 years later (Youniss & Yates, 1999).

STRENGTHS-BASED LEARNING

Why some young people become engaged while others show very little interest in society is the topic of much speculation and research. Two approaches to the problem are found in current literature. The dominant method uses a deficit reduction model, attempting to treat or control undesirable behaviors in young people. This approach focuses on risk avoidance, teaching skills for managing stress, regulating alcohol and drug usage, and curbing other objectionable activities of today's youth culture. My interest in youth civic engagement is anchored in a second approach, one that embraces the insights of positive youth development and the power of strengths-based experiential education (Damon, 2004; Larson, 2000; Lerner, 2007).

> While the positive approach recognizes the developmental challenges that young people face, it refuses to view the developmental process mainly as an effort to overcome deficits and risk. Instead, it emphasizes the manifest potential of youth—including those from the most disadvantaged backgrounds, as well as those with highly troubled personal histories. The positive youth approach aims at understanding, educating, and engaging children in productive activities rather than at correcting, curing, or treating them for maladaptive tendencies or so-called disabilities (Damon, 2008, p. 168).

The positive approach frames human development as the aim of education, and views parents, schools, and communities as partners in creating future citizens. This way of thinking asks the question: What fosters development?

ENGAGEMENT BEGINS IN CHILDHOOD

The United States depends on citizens who are engaged in nonprofit organizations, fundraising, volunteering, community leadership, policy-making, and problem-solving to fulfill its democratic ideals.

In 2008, the nation elected its first African American President. At the time, many saw this election as a turning point for the country and as an opportunity to address pressing issues of the times, including inequality, poverty, and the environment.

Millions of children and adolescents followed the presidential campaign in their homes and classrooms, more actively engaged in the process than ever before. But what experiences will sustain their engagement in future presidential races? What meaning will they derive from the challenges of actively participating in established community programs, leading efforts to challenge traditional thinking, or acting to solve the root causes of societal problems? How will their initiative be fostered by supportive adults?

The seeds of civic engagement are undoubtedly sown in childhood. Research shows that adolescents who express greater commitments to civic engagement are more engaged as adults (Kahne & Sporte, 2008; Youniss et al., 1997). But becoming an actively engaged citizen is not easy. In fact, there are many obstacles and challenges to overcome. Young people must learn how to think strategically, set goals, weigh choices, cope with disappointments, and take action—essential aspects of initiative. Understanding how these skills are developed through civic engagement is central to facilitating learning experiences that foster civic action.

As we attempt to understand how adolescents and young adults thrive as engaged citizens, we know that "circumstances matter" (Diener, 2009). We not only need to develop empathy and altruism in children, we need to provide the situations and experiences that enable them to turn empathy into positive social change. This means that traditional assumptions about youth community service and service-learning programs must be challenged to consider ways in which inner strengths, like initiative, are being developed.

To better understand the concept of initiative, the research presented in this book examines the lives of young people who have demonstrated initiative through civic engagement. This type of research, often called a *normative study*, typically challenges readers to change the way they think about an important belief or assumption (Thacher, 2006). What can we learn from a population that Damon (2008) identified as one of the smallest groups of today's purposeful youth that may help other young people become more actively engaged? Should we value the development of initiative in community service and service-learning programs? And if so, how would adults act in ways to encourage its development?

By studying the stories of highly engaged young adults who find meaning and purpose in political and societal causes, my research discovered more about the types of initiative-building experiences that help youth sustain involvement over time. Highly engaged youth have developed initiative for reasons not fully understood. The research described in this book goes beyond why young people become involved in civil society to the rich experiences and circumstances that form their ability and motivation to sustain civic action in the face of obstacles. The goal was to better understand how initiative toward active citizenship is fostered by the shared efforts of schools, families, and communities.

Numerous studies on youth civic engagement focus on increasing the number of youth participating in civic life in broad areas of involvement (Kahne & Sporte, 2008; Zukin et al., 2006). Others focus on examining specific youth activism programs, service-learning, or community service experiences and their developmental benefits for participants (Larson & Hansen, 2005; Youniss & Yates, 1996, 1997, 1999). My study engaged a diverse group of purposeful youth who had demonstrated long-term commitment and voluntary engagement in collective social or environmental efforts aimed at improving the lives of others in their communities or around the world and who had sustained their efforts for a minimum of three years.

> The purposeful are those who have found something meaningful to dedicate themselves to, who have sustained this interest over a period of time, and who express a clear sense of what they are trying to accomplish in the world and why. They have found a cause or ultimate goal that inspires their efforts from day to day and helps them fashion a coherent future agenda (Damon, 2008, p. 60).

By studying the lived experiences of purposeful youth, my research provides new insights into how initiative is nurtured through public service and how challenging civic learning experiences are transformed into sustained civic action. While interviews with young people focused on how they overcame the challenges of civic participation, those same conversations also showed that empathy and human connectedness were at the core of what motivated civically-engaged young people. It was their caring for others that drove their community and social change efforts over time.

EMPATHY-IN-ACTION

During the past two decades, studies show a substantial rise in self-centeredness and a decline in empathy among American youth (Konrath et al., 2011; Weissbourd & Jones, 2014). They also signal an era of lower community engagement and social advocacy by young people compared with previous generations. This research, and the questions it brings to mind, is deeply troubling and forces us to reflect on what has changed in America and what we have lost as a result.

But it also stirs us to ask: Can we reclaim the power of empathy in a more impersonal, fast-paced Digital Age? The answer is a resounding "yes!" In this book, young people themselves show us how, affirming why empathy is at the heart of human and societal success and well-being. It shows how we cultivate children's natural abilities to care and act on behalf of others. When we connect the power of empathy-based relationships with meaningful volunteer service, the results for kids and their communities can be transformative.

It is not surprising that people hunger for kinder, gentler times, when neighbors knew and cared about the kids next door and the word "bully" represented only a few students in a school. In spite of today's harsh and seemingly uncaring political climate, most people still feel comforted by the principles that made America great, of freedom, equality, and human rights.

Many resonate deeply with the founding American ideals that sought to relieve suffering and create a better world for everyone. We recall with fondness the "greatest generation" whom Tom Brokaw argued were men and women who did not fight for fame or recognition, but because it was the "right thing to do." Today, many wonder if those values and notions of success have been lost and whether we can instill them in new generations of children.

There is a common thread woven through these American memories. They remind us of a time when success was associated with what I call *empathy-in-action*. In other words, success was driven by much more than wealth, status, or even a college education. We "liked" people, not because of their popularity on social media, but because they were ethical people who demonstrated how much they cared about their neighbors, communities, and country. That spirit of caring was transformed into actions and innovations that not only made America great, but also brought tangible success to masses of its citizens. When did that notion of success become flawed? What have we lost because of it?

Authentic success can be linked to empathy-in-action throughout human history, and especially in the United States where empathy-driven volunteerism has flourished for several centuries. But somewhere in the past few decades, we have lost what it means to be guided by a greater good. We are raising and educating children to compete in an increasingly cut-throat, data-driven, and power-hungry world. As a result, there is a growing recognition that something worthwhile is missing from our lives and the lives of our children. That "something" is empathy.

Today, many acknowledge this loss. Public figures like Ariana Huffington launched a campaign to redefine success beyond money and power. In her book, *Thrive: The Third Metric to Redefining Success and Creating a Life of Well-Being, Wisdom, and Wonder* (2014), she speaks with passion about what we have lost and her personal quest to rediscover a more meaningful life. She is joined by business leaders like LinkedIn CEO Jeff Weiner who told an audience about his mission to "expand the world's collective wisdom and compassion." Top universities, including Stanford, have created centers to study altruism and to infuse businesses with empathy and compassion.

These quiet changes taking place in America's workplaces and universities reflect an effort to regain what's missing in our adult lives. Many companies who have embraced a broader definition of success have also adopted the concept of the *triple bottom line*. These are metrics that go beyond a simple profit and loss statement to include people and the planet. Many of these changes have been prompted by recent research showing when people care about each other they also contribute to the greater good of society. In the process, human health and well-being are vastly enriched.

While American companies explore the value of the triple bottom line and their commitments to social and environmental ideals, are we doing enough as parents, educators, and community leaders to make sure children become a vital part of those future workplaces?

Are we adequately preparing today's youth to become the caring and compassionate employees and citizens of tomorrow?

The simple answer is "no." And that's the reason for my research and this book. Through empathy, the brain is stimulated to learn new skills, producing a multiplier effect that increases children's resilience, self-awareness, and creativity, as well as a plethora of other abilities. When children learn to care, empathy not only drives their civic actions in the world, but also leads to personal fulfillment and life success. They become curious about learning, resourceful, and better able to live their values in everyday life. In the chapters that follow, young people share stories of how this happens through rich and meaningful service experiences.

I am contacted weekly by parents and teachers who feel helpless to change the current climate of how American children are raised and educated by data-driven metrics that are known to fuel self-centeredness. They mostly write to thank me for the research-based online articles I write, including my columns at RootsOfAction.com and Psychology Today.

They also share troubling insights. Here is an email I recently received from a career teacher in Virginia who gave me permission to reprint it, but asked to remain anonymous because he feared reprisal from school administrators:

> Thank you for being a dose of sanity during this tumultuous time in society. I have followed your research and publications, printed and quoted you many times to administrators, parents, and students.
>
> I am a child of parents who survived the Depression and World War II and they raised me to value hard work, setbacks, and to count my blessings. It was generally well-accepted among my students and parents until the past 15 years or so.
>
> Lately, there has been a huge rejection of developing character in stu-

dents. Parents, administrators and students are not allowed to fail. If we fail a student, they blame the teacher; make their life difficult; or worse, tie it to their evaluation and fire them.

Teachers receive edicts from central administration that we can't grade behaviors and can only use test scores. It's insane! As a public school teacher, I am not permitted to evaluate a student's hard work, perseverance, curiosity, caring, grit, honesty, etc. Yet, your research and others say it is one of the most important factors in success.

I just wanted to thank you for your contributions. There are a few of us seasoned educators left that are fighting the good fight. Let's hope we can turn this around.

This kind of feedback continues to drive my passion for writing on the topics of positive youth development and youth civic engagement—fields that are systemically interconnected. There is a groundswelling, grassroots imperative to "turn this around." But how?

The answers can be found through an understanding of how adults impact the healthy development of children and teens. When we cultivate empathy in kids, they learn to succeed in school and life. They are motivated from inside themselves to take action. Among other benefits, research shows empathy reduces prejudice, inequality, racism, and bullying; it increases the quality of our relationships, and promotes well-being. As young people transform empathy into action, they grow to become empowered citizens and leaders of tomorrow's companies, communities, and nations.

LEADERSHIP IN FUTURE DECADES

This book merges scientific evidence with the real life experiences of today's Millennial generation to call for changes in how we raise and educate kids to live and lead in future decades. For all of the differences in our melting pot of languages, religions, and political beliefs, humans share a number of neurobiological truths. Two of these truths are foundational to my research on civically-engaged youth:

1. Our brains are wired for empathy from birth, but do not form a lasting circuitry of caring without specific types of human interaction and practice.
2. Our relationships and experiences as children and teenagers profoundly impact how we feel and express empathy for the remainder of our lives.

The young people interviewed in the following chapters discovered lives of meaning through their innate, biological ability to feel empathy. Their journeys were not easy because forming caring relationships is not easy. They overcame difficult challenges in their lives with the help of parents, teachers, and other caring adults.

As those challenges were met, these young people developed skills, abilities, and knowledge that helped them find success in all aspects of life. Their new found abilities, like creativity, resilience, and resourcefulness, enabled them to become effective change makers—to play leadership roles in causes that spoke to their hearts.

Supporting recent brain research, their message is clear and convincing: the caring individuals they became were the product of their relationships and civic experiences. These two ingredients are the powerful common threads of their stories; threads that should be part of all children's stories.

Throughout much of American history, we have nurtured empathy to very high neurobiological levels. Not only have we raised and educated generations who cared for individuals, but we have also engaged their brains' ability to care for groups of people like immigrants, the homeless, or victims of abuse. One of the most important ways we've accomplished this is by engaging children and teens in age-appropriate volunteer experiences.

But volunteerism has changed in America. While the number of kids who volunteer has risen because of school requirements, recent studies show just how few find meaning and purpose through work in their communities (Damon (2008). For most, volunteerism has become just another high school requirement that bolsters a good college resume.

No one would disagree that volunteerism is a major asset to democracy and that caring for others is an important value to instill in children. But in an ardent effort to get large numbers of children and teens involved in service, we've overlooked a major aspect of brain development—how kids learn to care and how empathy positively impacts all aspects of life success, including civic life and leadership. The stories in this book illustrate these points. Young people themselves speak with a clear and united voice: "Yes, it is possible to develop caring leaders in the Digital Age. And here are the ways adults help and hinder us."

NUMBERS VERSUS LEARNING

Over the past several decades, American volunteerism has become a big industry focused on numbers. Nonprofits compete for charitable dollars based on how many Twitter or Facebook followers they have achieved or how many thousands of young people show up at huge fundraising events. This data-driven approach that ostensibly helps teach American youth to care for others should not surprise us. It mirrors strategies used in other areas of our educational system. It is part of a culture that values numbers over learning.

Driven by test scores and grades, we take pride in seeing kids achieve by the numbers rather than through their abilities to glean meaning, understanding, and purpose from their schooling experiences. Because numbers are easier to quantify, it has become the major method of evaluating our success as parents and teachers. But this approach, now being challenged by many of today's educational leaders, does not support what we know about child and adolescent development. In fact, studies in neurobiology show that these practices actually diminish children's abilities to care for each other and the greater good.

Misled by the benefits of "big picture data," we have focused on broad statistics rather than individual learning. We feel good with the knowledge that 70% of teenagers volunteer today. Though when we look deeply into the research, we must reluctantly acknowledge that most are occasional volunteers—kids who sign up for brief jobs who are motivated by high school resumes, peer pressure, or the latest social media effort. Of those teens who volunteer, we also know that only 18% perform acts of service on a regular basis. And perhaps the most discouraging research of all, William Damon, PhD, of Stanford University, found that less than 2% of teens find purpose through community service.

Is volunteerism really helping kids develop higher levels of empathy? Or are we teaching them to persevere in a competitive system that rewards hours rather than meaning? This book dives into these and other important questions, challenging us to ask how we can bring more purpose and meaning to children's lives.

The Digital Age has changed the ways we engage with others and placed more focus on individual accomplishments. The lives of most children and teens are intricately woven with the latest social media trends. Whether kids measure their success through "likes" on Facebook, "favorites" on Twitter, or "likes" on Instagram, the average American child spends more than seven hours a day engaged with "entertainment media" instead of relating with people face-to-face.

In an increasingly data-driven society, children receive more external than internal rewards for their accomplishments. According to neuroscience, this profoundly reduces their levels of empathy.

CROSSING ACADEMIC DISCIPLINES

The stories in this book challenge us to think differently about how we teach kids to care from kindergarten through college, and how volunteerism can play an important role in helping young people attain higher levels of empathy and initiative to drive social change. To do so, it engages students who have found meaning through civic engagement and gives voice to their powerful stories. It reveals the experiences that shaped the caring and committed young adults they became. These young people help answer questions including:

- What skills and traits help children become compassionate caregivers and citizens?

- How are these skills developed during childhood and adolescence?

- How do young people find meaning through service experiences?

- How do adults support children's learning through empathy-based relationships?

- What kinds of environments transform young people into social justice advocates?

- How does the ability to care stimulate the growth of other life skills?

It's time to reverse the trend toward self-centeredness and individualism, and expand what we know about caring from the experiences of digital natives themselves. Participating in service projects from young ages can influence children to care, but only when they are enriched by supportive relationships with adults, positive values, mentoring, and age-appropriate opportunities that reflect what we know about neurobiology and human development. With that knowledge, we can help today's young people develop into caring individuals and engaged citizens capable of taking on the challenging social and environmental tasks ahead.

To a great extent, researchers who study how children develop into caring adults and engaged citizens do so in isolated fields of study, including child and adolescent development, affective neuroscience, psychology, civic engagement, and political science. But increasingly, those fields are overlapping one another.

For example, researchers at CIRCLE (The Center for Information & Research on Civic Learning and Engagement) who study youth voting and political participation are more likely to acknowledge the tenets of child and adolescent development when analyzing political and social trends. Likewise, those studying youth development consider today's political issues, educational climate, and digital lifestyles as backdrops for how young people are motivated to act in caring ways. The field of neuroscience is beginning to support research in these neighboring fields as well, providing more and more evidence of how we nurture kids who care.

This book utilizes multidisciplinary research to better understand the lived experiences of civically-engaged youth. Two strands of literature offer insights into this population. The first is the literature on child and adolescent development, particularly the theoretical underpinnings of identity and initiative. The second is the literature on youth civic engagement, including the experiences that positively influence civic involvement, help adolescents navigate the challenges and obstacles of volunteerism, and provide opportunities for open social/political discussions and reflection.

Recent studies have questioned adolescent motivation for civic engagement. Some suggest many students participate in community service because of a desire to look good on college applications (Davila & Mora, 2007; Friedland & Morimoto, 2005; Schneider & Stevenson, 1999). With an extraordinary pressure to attain success, many high-achieving youth see civic activities as a normalized expectation. Even middle-achievers see college within their reach only if they do enough of the right volunteer activities (Friedland & Morimoto, 2005).

This book examines a population of young people who began volunteering in high school, then sustained that commitment into their college years. Probing into the inherent conflicts between self and society, as well as how young people develop initiative through internal versus external rewards, sheds light on why some students sustain civic engagement and others do not.

What we are beginning to piece together by crossing academic disciplines has the potential to change the way we raise and educate children who care for others and give back to their communities in the Digital Age. Narrative research is known for its ability to understand the mysteries of human development from an inter-disciplinary perspective rather than merely quantifying or comparing numerical data.

By studying the stories of young people who became recognized for their generosity and acts of caring, we are better able to understand and compare the similarities among them. In the process, we enable youth to tell us what helps them in today's world, complete with its modern, quirky, and everyday challenges.

This qualitative approach to research, combined with rich storytelling, is the foundation of this book. Everyone relates to stories. We gain insights from them in ways quantitative research cannot alone provide. That's why the voices of these young people are front and center. They are powerful voices by themselves, but their stories take on greater importance as we link them to the latest research in inter-disciplinary fields of study.

THE VALUE OF MENTORSHIP

Our brains are hardwired to care, but they do not remain that way without real-world practice and empathy-based relationships throughout adolescence; yet we continue to assume that going to the right schools and getting resumes filled with volunteer service will somehow produce caring kids. The young people in this book challenge these beliefs and assumptions. They cause us to take notice of how we parent, teach, and mentor them to be their best selves.

For example, Scott, a 20-year-old Black student at Nyack College in New York, grew up in North Carolina's tobacco country. Recalling his teenage years, he said, "I was very shy, very quiet. And I didn't really care about getting involved in my community." But in ninth grade, he learned of an organization in Durham that was "looking for youth to go out and speak to other youth about tobacco and smoking." Scott confessed, "I always knew that smoking was bad, but I didn't really know or care much about it."

Scott said he was attracted to working for this organization because it wasn't the typical kind of menial work where adults tell you what to do. "The fact that it was youth to youth was a huge draw," he said. When I pressed him to dig deeper into other factors that motivated him to get involved, he admitted, "They made it seem like you didn't have to be perfect, that they would help you. I thought that was cool—they met me at my own level." Trying hard to give me further insight, Scott added, "I also thought it would force me to stretch my rubber band a little bit—to stretch my boundaries."

As Scott recalled his work with the anti-smoking campaign, he spoke highly of Bonnie, the adult leader. "She let youth play a huge role," he said. For example, she involved them in decision-making and with training other young people. With an air of pride in his voice, Scott said, "She gave us guidance, but left the control to us. That's what works when you're trying to motivate youth. You've got to make them feel like they've got some type of role and some importance. That's what Bonnie did."

With Scott's shy and reserved personality and lack of interest in community activities, most parents and teachers would not have predicted that this ninth grader would grow to lead a national anti-tobacco campaign, be awarded $100,000 for his cause, and speak to Congress and thousands of teenagers throughout the country. Scott's story is just one of many in this book that show how mentoring relationships with adults combined with meaningful service is an essential part of how American youth learn to care about others and the world around them. Ironically, it is also how they learn to succeed in an increasingly interconnected, hi-tech society.

SERVICE REQUIRES INNER STRUGGLE

For many young people, service is an easy, meaningless, and often-required obligation of growing up in the U.S. But the young people in this book demonstrate that service should not be easy, or a simple series of activities on the journey toward college. They believe caring and service requires internal struggle to make it part of who you are rather than what you do. They claim that without the educators and other adults who influenced their lives, they would not have had transformative volunteer experiences. And without those relationships and experiences, they would not have become caring, engaged young adults.

The young voices throughout these chapters share strong messages that improve our understanding of what it really takes to teach kids to give back to society in this fast-moving, more impersonal Digital Age. Common themes about relationships and service experiences emerge from young people in more than 20 U.S. states who have a wide diversity of ethnicity, religions, and political affiliations. Stories are told by immigrants, by children raised in single-parent and traditional households, and by students like Scott who never dreamed of the futures they now hold. Whether they were raised wealthy or poor, they had strikingly common types of adult support and life-changing service experiences as tweens and teens.

Young people share important childhood experiences, turning points, how adults supported their journeys, and how they acquired a deep sense of caring. Their stories are inspirational and instructive. They force us to take notice of what matters most. Even as society marches toward increased emphasis on knowledge, information, and technological innovation, these young people believe caring must continue to be part of America's culture and social history.

THE SCIENCE OF YOUTH DEVELOPMENT

If we want children to grow into citizens who are willing to help neighbors, organize food drives, or lead initiatives that solve root causes of societal problems, we need to understand the science of youth development and how empathy gets transformed into action. In the past several decades, neuroscience has discovered the critical importance of mother-child emotional bonding, also known as attachment, in the very early years of life. Many books have been written about how the preschool years influence children's future relationships, including their abilities to care, empathize, and feel compassion for others.

While these early years are critical to healthy child development, more recent studies in affective neurobiology show us that caring neurons must be stimulated throughout childhood and adolescence. As the stories in this book illustrate, this happens at all developmental levels, from elementary school through college, with the teen years being particularly important as young people internalize what it means to care and begin to identify themselves as caring persons.

Learning to care happens everywhere, including home, school, faith-based programs, after-school activities, volunteer projects, and service-learning. Who is most likely to stand up for someone being bullied or unjustly marginalized by society? Who is most likely to solve the social and environmental problems of tomorrow? Why do caring young people also thrive in life? What can each of us do to mentor a child, or a whole generation of them, toward the life they were meant to lead?

The answers to these questions and more are found in stories told by Scott and other adolescents in this book. Particularly touching story lines include how Ashley, a young woman raised with minimum resources and whose cocaine-addicted father was in jail most of her life, found meaning in comforting dying patients and their families. They include Giovanni, a young man raised in an extraordinarily wealthy family, who tells how he left the world of comfort and luxury, and found purpose in helping people who were living in poverty.

Their stories are success stories, not because of the grades, trophies, or awards most sought after in today's society, but because of the people they became—young adults whose caring spirits and meaningful goals fueled civic actions in the world. Whether they attended public or elite private schools, each developed a commitment to helping others. Their stories should be more commonplace. With the support of families, schools, and communities, they can be.

Acts of kindness, empathy, and compassion are essential to healthy communities. The young people who participated in my research study were a diverse group of 18- to 22-year-olds. They talk about how these human abilities were instilled in them as children and how their capacity to care contributed to the young adults they became. The group talks of their struggles to become caring individuals during their teen years—when it's not often seen as "cool" to show you care about anyone. And they talk about how their feelings toward others eventually overpowered the pressure they felt to be like many of their peers.

BOOK AUDIENCE AND CHAPTER SUMMARIES

This book is written for educators, youth mentors, parents, coaches, clergy, psychologists, policymakers, and other community leaders who share a commitment to educating and raising kids who give back to others and who work collaboratively to solve the issues facing society. It will be of particular interest to leaders who work in education and youth development as well as those who work more broadly toward democracy, equity, social justice, and environmental sustainability.

In brief, the following are summaries of remaining chapters. Depending upon your interests, feel free to dive into chapters in whatever order best suits your needs.

Chapter 2 provides an introduction to the research on youth civic engagement and why a broad perspective is essential, particularly for nonprofit organizations, schools, and youth service programs that want to understand how research supports their efforts to foster engaged, innovative, and committed young citizens.

Chapter 3 examines scientific background about storytelling and how narrative research helps us understand the lived experiences of civically-engaged youth. Here, readers are introduced to the stories and backgrounds of the young people who contributed to this book.

Chapter 4 introduces five themes that emerged from surveys and interviews with civically-engaged youth, including reflections in young people's own voices.

Chapter 5 explores a handful of representative stories in depth that characterize a process of transformative learning, common to all the youth in my study.

Chapter 6 introduces *The Compass Advantage*™ framework of eight core abilities that enable young people to chart successful courses in life. It explores how adult mentors foster these abilities, helping youth believe in themselves and learn to contribute to their communities.

Chapter 7 reviews the three main findings from the research study with civically-engaged youth, including what the findings mean for how we teach, parent, and mentor children on their pathways toward active citizenship.

A CALL TO ACTION

I hope this book is a thought-provoking call to action—a moral imperative to rethink how we teach kids to care in a more hurried, impersonal, and data-driven generation. It is meant to educate, inspire, and bring attention to the relationships and experiences in childhood and adolescence that shape caring and community-minded adults. It demonstrates both the complexity and simplicity of this process and shines a light on why we should reclaim the power of empathy, compassion, and meaningful civic engagement for a new generation.

Today's young people rely on their families, schools, and communities to provide the life experiences, skills, and relationships that foster their abilities to create a caring and compassionate world for themselves and future generations. When self-centeredness among

American youth is rising and few are finding meaning through volunteerism, we have a duty to ask why.

Rather than placing blame on today's youth culture or the Digital Age, it is time to look at how adults can step up, take responsibility, and nurture children's natural abilities to care for individuals and societies. Powerful empathy-based relationships combined with meaningful youth service experiences played a huge role in developing the caring, engaged young people depicted in this book.

What stands out is how all of us can help nurture kids to become their best selves through their natural ability to care. If these kinds of relationships and experiences are harnessed for millions of young people, we will reclaim an important part of our culture as Americans and also feel an unshakable hope in the future.

2

A Broad Perspective

He who loves practice without theory is like the sailor who boards ship without a rudder and compass and never knows where he may cast.

— Leonardo da Vinci

My research on civically-engaged youth focused on understanding how young people sustain *initiative* for social and environmental causes over time, despite the challenges. This chapter explores initiative in a larger context, including motivation, ideology, purpose, and other aspects that help define a young person's civic identity and drive to work toward the betterment of society.

Why this larger perspective? Every research study fits into a much bigger body of knowledge. That knowledge provides a compass in which to ask new questions and a basis on which to turn theory into practice. Good research should measure itself against previous research, comparing and contrasting what was gained and what still needs to be learned.

As a fellow at the Institute for Social Innovation at Fielding Graduate University, I currently study the developmental aspects of how young people thrive in life and how empathy-driven civic engagement contributes to that thriving. With each new study I review, I always attempt to put it in context with what the scholarly community already knows.

This larger perspective is particularly essential to nonprofit organizations, schools, and youth service programs that want to understand how research supports their efforts in the real world. This broader knowledge should become a driving force in program development and strategic planning. It is also critical for funding proposals, where it is necessary to show that a program, course, or service experience is supported by research and that adult leaders understand youth development in a broad context.

This chapter provides an appreciative assessment of the current thinking on youth civic engagement, including leading definitions, concepts, assumptions, and theories. It explores the underpinnings of adolescent identity development and the relationship of identity to civic initiative.

THE NEED FOR SYNTHESIS

The scholarly conversations about youth civic engagement cross many disciplines, including social psychology, adolescent development, education, positive psychology, political science, sociology, philosophy, neurobiology, and theology. Since John Dewey (1916) first linked youth experiences in a school community with the development of capacities for democratic living, civic-learning and service opportunities for young people have flourished.

Not only have youth contributed to society with volunteer hours, many scholars also attribute their civic engagement experiences to positive gains in development, including the development of identity, empathy, moral character, initiative, self-efficacy, and agency. Forty years after Dewey, Erikson (1968) contended that identity was situated in both the core of the individual and in the heart of the culture surrounding the individual. The recurrent theme of his work was that childhood and adolescence not only affected an individual's later life, but the life of society itself (Erikson, 1950).

Not surprisingly, research in the field of youth civic engagement has taken two main paths. Social psychologists, political scientists, and sociologists have studied social, political, and generational differences among youth to learn how key events and contexts of young people's lives are important to understanding engagement (Levine, 2007; Zukin et al., 2006).

Other researchers, particularly in the field of developmental psychology, have studied the developmental factors that made civic engagement especially important as young people progressed through their formative years. These developmental studies focused on ideas such as political-moral identity, social responsibility, and purpose. Generally, they support Erikson's (1968) view that young people need to find meaning as they establish their individual identity within the societal framework (Damon, Menon, & Bronk, 2003; Youniss, 2006).

While the study of the individual and the study of societal contexts are both essential to understanding youth civic engagement, there is a general lack of synthesis of the two approaches. Without such integration, an incomplete educational agenda exists. Through the study of adolescents' lived experiences, my research used a multidisciplinary approach to explore both the individual and contextual influences on sustained civic action.

There is strong evidence that positive learning experiences play a key role in developing civically-engaged young people. Therefore, this chapter explores a number of research studies for their contributions, methodologies, outcomes, and limitations. To bridge the gap between civic learning and civic action, civic initiative-building experiences must be better understood.

DEMOCRATIC ENGAGEMENT

Before we can understand how young people are motivated to sustain civic engagement over time, it is important to define the types of engagement required by an effective democracy. While most of the scholarly literature defines engagement in broad terms, three categories of engagement are pertinent to this book: civic engagement, political engagement, and cognitive engagement.

Zukin et al. (2006) defined civic engagement as "participation aimed at achieving a public good . . . through direct hands-on work in cooperation with others" (p. 51). This type of engagement, usually performed through nongovernmental organizations within one's own community, includes wide-ranging actions and behaviors. For example, activities may vary from volunteering at a food bank to organizing a food drive, from participating in a clean-up campaign, to leading an effort to install solar panels on school buildings.

Political engagement was defined by Verba, Schlozman, and Brady (1995) as an "activity that has the intent or effect of influencing government action—either directly by affecting the making or implementation of public policy or indirectly by influencing the selection of people who make those policies" (p. 38). These types of activities include working on campaigns, boycotting, protesting, circulating petitions, and producing art, poetry, or writing with social themes. Since social and environmental issues often evoke political activism, it is important to examine how young people are inspired to transfer their volunteer passions into the political realm.

Zukin et al. (2006) also identified areas of cognitive engagement important to democracy. This type of engagement is associated with activities that include following what is going on in government and public affairs, talking with family and friends about social and political issues, and paying attention to current news and information. Cognitive engagement may help sustain civic commitment. My research explored how young people think critically about social, political, and economic problems beyond surface causes and how adults support them in this process.

HOW CITIZENS SUPPORT SOCIETY

While categories of engagement are important to define, it is also important to distinguish the types of citizens that support an effective democratic society. Westheimer and Kahne (2004) outlined three categories of citizens that civics education programs aim to develop: the personally responsible citizen, the participatory citizen, and the justice-oriented citizen. Their framework highlighted core assumptions and important differences in how civics education is envisioned. Each type of citizen engenders a divergent set of theoretical and programmatic goals. These visions of citizenship are not hierarchical. For example, personally responsible citizens do not necessarily develop into participatory citizens or justice-oriented citizens. Programs that promote one type of citizen are generally quite different from one another and draw on distinct core beliefs. Westheimer and Kahne's three citizen-types are summarized below.

1. Personally Responsible Citizens

When we envision *personally responsible citizens,* we think of conscientious people with good character. They have integrity and are law-abiding members of communities. They are likely to vote in local and national elections and volunteer to help out in times of crisis. They may contribute to food drives or give money to local causes.

According to Westheimer and Kahne, activities and youth programs that seek to develop personally responsible citizens focus almost entirely on character-building. They stress morality, self-discipline, individual responsibility, integrity, honesty, compassion, and respect. Character education is the most popular type of youth development program in America.

Westheimer and Kahne (2004) posited that developing the personally responsible citizen is "an inadequate response to the challenges of educating a democratic citizenry" (p. 243). While there is agreement that character traits such as integrity, self-responsibility, and honesty are vital to communities, these programs diminish the importance of collective initiative and distract attention from finding systemic solutions to root societal problems (Barber, 1992; Boyte, 1991, 2005; Kahne & Westheimer, 2006).

2. Participatory Citizens

People who are considered *participatory citizens* hold leadership positions in communities. They join local organizations and boards. These citizens know how government agencies and nonprofits work, and they understand the strategies for getting things done. They are more likely to organize a food drive, register people to vote, or raise funds for local causes.

Goals of youth programs that develop participatory citizens facilitate student engagement in cooperative, community-based efforts. Program emphasis is on leadership, organization, and problem-solving skills.

3. Justice-Oriented Citizens

People who work to examine and solve the root causes of societal problems are referred to as *justice-oriented citizens*. They see beyond surface causes to the systemic implications for multiple sectors of society and seek to address perceived injustices. These citizens go beyond traditional leadership roles to question, debate, and change structural patterns. They start social movements and effect systemic change.

Training for justice-oriented citizens is much less common in America. Programs to develop this type of citizen involve students in collective efforts within their communities and encourage young people to critically think about the root causes of social injustices. These programs do not view volunteerism or charity as an end in itself; rather, they aim to teach students how to bring about systemic change that improves the lives of impoverished and marginalized populations.

Volunteer service in America today has been segregated from the concept of citizenship, and the distinction between moral development and citizenship development has been blurred. This line of thinking may offer insight into why young people are considered disengaged in democratic society at the same time that traditional volunteerism is at an all-time high.

THE INTERCONNECTED NATURE OF CITIZENSHIP

While Westheimer and Kahne's (2004) framework provides a helpful way to differentiate types of citizens, it does not reflect a systemic understanding of citizenship. The model does not acknowledge the interconnected nature of citizenship, or how, for example, justice-oriented citizens might also work within established systems. The labels lead to some confusion as well, since all citizens can be deemed to be participatory. Entrepreneurial and grassroots efforts, an important aspect of citizenship, are missing from the model.

My work and research supports the view that civic education is the shared responsibility of families, schools, and community institutions. We must look at citizenship systemically, exploring multiple experiences, relationships, and contexts that not only propel young people to participate in democratic processes, but to become innovators for social change. The life stories of civically-engaged youth help inform this systemic view.

Westheimer and Kahne's (2004) framework contributed to my research because it made a clear distinction between those who act out of concern for other human beings alone and those who become participatory actors within a democracy. The core assumptions of each type of citizenry characterize common worldviews held by educators, parents, and many community organizations. My work extends Westheimer and Kahne's model by examining, through lived experiences, how young people develop the initiative to act on their feelings, assumptions, and worldviews.

To better connect civic engagement to the goals of a participatory democracy, my research focused on adolescent involvement in areas outside altruistic service or responsible citizenship alone. While honoring the importance of character and moral development to society, it supports Boyte's (2005) contention that a shift in the meaning of civic agency is necessary. Citizens need to be envisioned beyond their actions as individual voters or volunteers. They are co-creators of democracy and we need to understand how young people become motivated to lead and organize citizen action, overcome obstacles, understand different perspectives, analyze established systems, and solve the root causes of social and environmental problems. Barber (1992) acknowledged the importance of this shift:

The literacy required to live in civil society, the competence to participate in democratic communities, the ability to think critically and act
deliberately in a pluralistic world, the empathy that permits us to hear
and thus accommodate others, all involve skills that must be acquired. . .
. The democratic faith is rooted in the belief that all humans are capable
of such excellence and have not just the right but the capacity to become
citizens. (pp. 4-5)

For the purposes of my study, the term *civic engagement* was used
broadly to include civic, political, and cognitive engagement. A systemic view of engagement includes the study of patterns and relationships between types of engagement rather than studying or promoting one type over another. By focusing on highly engaged youth
who fall into the broad categories of Westheimer and Kahne's (2004)
participatory and justice-oriented citizens, my study explored how
young people move beyond empathy and altruistic acts to acquire the
initiative and skills necessary to engage in participatory democratic
processes.

DEVELOPING A CIVIC IDENTITY

To explore how young people construct an identity that incorporates
sustained civic engagement, an understanding of the developing adolescent is essential. The work of Erik Erikson (1950, 1968) is not
only distinguished for its broad theoretical framework on understanding human development, but for its insights on adolescent identity formation and other psychosocial constructs that contribute to
the cumulative aspect of development. In his groundbreaking book,
Childhood and Society, Erikson (1950) introduced his "Eight Stages of
Man" (p. 247) beginning with infancy and ending with old age. The
following table describes the conflicts to be resolved at each stage
of the life cycle, emerging values, and general period of life broadly
associated with each phase of maturation (Stevens-Long & Commons, 1992).

Erikson's Eight Stages of Life

Conflict at each stage	Emerging value	Period of life
Basic trust vs. mistrust – Consistency, continuity, and comfort produce a feeling of security and predictability.	Hope	Infancy
Autonomy vs. shame and doubt – Parental firmness allows for the experience of demand fulfillment with limits that produce self-control.	Will	Early Childhood
Initiative vs. guilt – The development of the superego and cooperation with others support the growth of planning and a sense of responsibility.	Purpose	Play Age
Industry vs. inferiority – Working and learning with others produces skill and the ability in using tools, and weapons, and method, as well as feelings of self-esteem	Competence	School Age
Identity vs. role confusion – The physical changes of adolescence arouse a new search for sameness and continuity and the need for a coherent sense of self.	Fidelity	Adolescence
Intimacy vs. isolation – A new ability to tolerate the threat of ego loss permits the establishment of mature relationships involving the fusion and counterpointing of identity.	Love	Young Adulthood
Generativity vs. stagnation – The adult need to care for children and to guide the next generation produces the desire to leave something of substance as a legacy.	Care	Maturity
Integrity vs. despair – An accrued sense of order and meaning allows one to defend one's own life cycle as a contribution to the maintenance of the human world.	Wisdom	Old Age

From *Adult Life: Developmental Processes*, 4th ed. (p. 61), by Judith Stevens-Long and Michael L. Commons, 1992, Mountain View, CA: Mayfield Publishing. Reprinted with permission.

Although Erikson's (1950) theory was clearly stage-oriented, Erikson warned that charts and stage-like tools were designed as guides, not prescriptions. Each stage was not an achievement to be mastered, but rather a struggle for meaningful existence in which individuals engaged continuously, even as they approached death. With the completion of each stage, basic virtues emerged, essential qualities of the human spirit that passed from one generation to the next. These virtues included hope, will, purpose, competence, fidelity, love, care, and wisdom.

Erikson (1950) insisted that childhood and adolescence had lasting effects on the individual and on the whole of society. Research in civic engagement has shown this to be true. Young people who engage in their communities are more likely to become civically-engaged adults who contribute to society's thriving (Kahne & Sporte, 2008; Youniss, 2006; Youniss et al., 1997; Youniss & Yates, 1999). Erikson did not believe his stages of development represented specific age periods, but envisioned they would be revisited throughout life. Keeping Erikson's warnings in mind, this study drew from important concepts found in his third, fourth, and fifth stages of development and their relationship to sustained civic engagement in adolescence.

Erikson's (1950) third stage involved the formation of initiative versus guilt, and the basic virtues of inner and outer direction and purpose. Initiative, he said, was a "miracle of vigorous unfolding" (p. 255), suggesting that initiative development began in the third stage of life, but continued throughout all stages of life. Erikson described initiative as the process of "undertaking, planning and attacking a task" (p. 255). He also acknowledged that the undertaking involved an emotional "fumbling and fear" (p. 255), a process of stumbling, overcoming obstacles, and making adjustments. While this process, according to Erikson, began in preschool-age children, several studies found this process particularly relevant in a study of adolescents who participated in structured after-school voluntary activities (Larson, 2000; Larson & Hansen, 2005).

Erikson (1950) was quick to explain that initiative should not be confused with industriousness or the competitiveness associated with Western capitalism. Instead, he insisted that initiative was needed in all aspects of life and work, from "fruit-gathering to a system of enterprise" (p. 255). Erikson also discussed initiative within the context of moral responsibility, asserting the potential for transformation or destruction. He affirmed that adults fostered the development of initiative in children and acknowledged it as an important stepping stone to his fourth stage of industry versus inferiority.

Initiative development has been studied during adolescence and linked to volunteer civic experiences and programs (Larson & Hansen, 2005; Larson, Hansen, & Walker, 2005). Recent studies pointed to the significance of purpose and moral development during adolescence and correlated these concepts with civic engagement (Damon, 2008; Damon et al., 2003; Schneider & Stevenson, 1999). This research not only validates the importance of Erikson's construct of initiative to understanding what fosters and sustains civic engagement, but also suggests its relevance during the years of adolescence.

In his fourth stage, Erikson (1950) claimed that children learned to get recognition by producing things, developing a sense of industry versus inferiority. They discovered how to plan and construct things "beside and with others" (p. 260), profit from teachers, and emulate role models. In Western societies, this involves formal education, an indirect opportunity to practice productivity through performance. In this period, children developed a sense of opportunity differences. Some do better work than others. Erikson pointed out a danger that affected all of society when children feel the color of their skin, the culture of their parents, or the kinds of clothes they wear are more important than their will to learn. And he warned of another threat.

Children can focus on work to the exclusion of other life goals, such as the importance of relationship, love, caring, and compassion. This threat may be manifest when young people view community service as a way of demonstrating achievement and as a necessary route for college admission (Davila & Mora, 2007; Friedland & Morimoto, 2005).

Erikson (1950) pointed out that the more complicated the society, the greater the challenge of developing both industry and initiative. He said, "The more confusing specialization becomes . . . the more indistinct are the eventual goals of initiative; and the more complicated social reality, the vaguer are the father's and mother's role in it" (p. 259). In Erikson's lifetime, he could not possibly have imagined the complexity of today's global society. No longer do children follow in the careers of their parents or even begin to understand multifaceted job specialization at a young age. Today's complex knowledge society may delay the development of Erikson's constructs of initiative and industry such that they play more significant roles in the process of identity formation itself.

Adolescence is at the core of Erikson's (1950) fifth stage, identity versus role confusion. Everything before this time prepared a young person for more expansive social roles and finding who they were within a psychosocial context. For Erikson, these two identities joined together at adolescence, a uniting of self and society. This period drew on prior strengths, using them to face subsequent challenges. Ideology and values were confronted and affirmation by peers was important. In this period, young people defined differences between good and evil and developed a sense of morality that remained with them for a lifetime.

While Erikson explored the inner path of identity development in compelling ways, he also spoke to the social aspects of identity. As youth focused inward to discover self, they also looked outward to form a relationship with society and its traditions, forming an "inner solidarity with a group's ideals and identity" (Erikson, 1958, p. 109). This process of placing oneself in a social-historical context is important to the study of youth civic engagement, and researchers often use Erikson's stage of adolescent identity development as a framework for understanding the development of civic identity. For example, Yates and Youniss (1996) applied this stage of Erikson's theory to concepts of agency, moral-political awareness, and social relatedness.

Erikson (1968) made repeated use of the term *ideology* in his examination of identity, denoting "a universal psychological need for a system of ideas that provides a convincing world image" (p. 31). While contemporary civil society embraced a multitude of diverse worldviews and values, Erikson saw ideology as a way for teenagers to simplify, understand, and organize their experiences. With an ideological point of view, "a million daily tasks and transactions fall into practical patterns and spontaneous ritualization which can be shared by leaders and led, men and women, adults and children" (p.32). Ideology provided the social bond that permitted identity to transcend the individual and become part of the collective society.

In his essay on the life of George Bernard Shaw, Erikson demonstrated how ideology and identity were complementary, how ideology provided a way of making meaning from life experiences. Erikson cited religion, political beliefs, and ethnic affiliations as several traditional sources of ideology. He argued that young people seek ideology as part of the identity-formation process. Studies in youth civic engagement confirm the importance of ideology and its role in acting collaboratively to construct a better world (Youniss & Yates, 1999; Zukin et al., 2006).

During adolescence, Erikson (1968) asserted that young people explored various identities. During identity development, teens came to terms with crises of earlier years before taking their place in society. The adolescent looked for people and causes in which to have faith, and to serve worthwhile purposes. Erikson claimed, "The great governor of initiative is *conscience* . . . the ontogenetic cornerstone of morality (p. 119). He suggested that under-developed initiative would have consequences during adolescence, indicating teens may become self-restrictive and not live up to their potential. Or, they may overcompensate by displaying tireless initiative at any cost.

These consequences occurred when young people saw their worth in terms of what they were going to become in the future instead of what they are in the present. This scenario, Erikson argued, created embodied strain and stress. Research demonstrates potential consequences of under-developed initiative, finding pressured young people padding college admission resumes with volunteer activities (Friedland & Morimoto, 2005). While this activity cannot be correlated with a single cause or presumed to devalue volunteerism, its relationship to initiative development is an important topic to investigate.

Despite widespread use and acceptance of Erikson's (1950) theory of development, there are important challenges to his thinking. For example, Gilligan (1982) argued that identity is gender specific, pointing to differences in modes of thinking as well as differences in life crises between males and females. Because women have more innate concern for caring and compassion than men, their identity process differed.

The point is not that the male and female drive toward identity differed, but that the timing and dimensions were not the same. In fact, the literature on youth civic engagement confirms that adolescent females participate in community service at higher rates than males (Davila & Mora, 2007; Zukin et al., 2006). Cote and Levine (2002) also argued that Erikson's eight stages represented masculine, European experience and could not be generalized to ethnic minorities.

Some consider Erikson's theory out of date due to substantial changes in society since the 1960s. Berk (2007) considered the formal period of adolescence to be from the ages of 11 to 18. But because today's young people living in Western societies often delay marriage, extend formal education, and explore numerous career options, some researchers now consider adolescence to be much longer, often stretching into the early 20s (Dahl, 2004).

Discussions related to the definition of age periods are used to challenge Erikson's thinking despite the fact he never attributed ages to his model. Instead, researchers who followed Erikson attempted to link stages with age periods, leading to some confusion. Erikson's theory, when used as a broader guide to development to which it was intended, may be more helpful to the study of adolescents and young adults.

Erikson's views on identity development have undergone much challenge and reformulation since they were written and researchers have constructed their own meaning from his work (Friedman, 1999). Many disagree with the assumption that identity evolves in a progressive direction and, in fact, posit it is as likely to be regressive (van Hoof, 1999). Erikson's stage theory may imply that people naturally move from one stage to the next. This may be true for biological maturity or language acquisition, but other aspects of identity require experiences, opportunities, and positive circumstances—the social component of Erikson's psycho-social model. This is likely the case with civic identity. Flanagan (2003) argued that an exploration of political engagement must include a developmental perspective—one that examines the contexts and relationships of the formative years.

Erikson's model has provided a useful framework for understanding the development of civic engagement in young people (e.g., Damon et al., 2003; Pancer, Pratt, Hunsberger, & Alisat, 2007; Youniss &

Yates, 1997). A broad search of the literature found over 800 articles and studies on youth civic engagement that drew from Erikson's stages of adolescent development. His theory of identity, the subject of "more than five hundred published studies and over one thousand dissertations" (Marcia, 2004, p. 48) provides much empirical validation of its usefulness.

In order for youth to develop a civic identity they must reach a point of *identity achievement*, a process described in James Marcia's (1966) elaboration of Erikson's model. Marcia believed that the identity crisis is resolved and commitment emerged in late adolescence. It was during this time of commitment that adolescents dedicated themselves to social and political causes, the legacy of which sustained engagement over a lifetime.

> Individuals who construct their identity, modifying or rejecting some conferred elements, also possess a sense of having participated in a *self-initiated* and self-directed process. They know not only who they are, they know how they became that, and that they had a hand in the becoming. Furthermore, they have developed skills useful in the adaptive process of further self-construction and self-definition. (Marcia, Matteson, Oriofsky, Waterman, & Archer, 1993, p. 8)

James Marcia's many years of research into Erikson's theory emphasized the importance of identity as a self-initiated process. He reiterated that "at any given age period; one is dealing with eight psychosocial issues, in some form, not just one" (Marcia, 2004, p. 51). This understanding reinforces the importance of examining civic engagement in young people beyond the limits of identity development, to ask the question, "What fosters initiative?"

SUSTAINING INITIATIVE

While Erikson's (1950) theory lays a foundation for studying initiative within a psychosocial framework, other researchers and theorists have confirmed its multidimensional nature, importance during adolescence, and lifespan implications. Research that sheds light on the understanding of initiative comes from different epistemological traditions including psychosocial theory, social cognitive theory, and personality theory. Researchers in these fields relate initiative to numerous other constructs including self-efficacy, agency, self-regulation, autonomy, and intrinsic motivation.

Although the word has its root in *initiate*, it means much more than the ability to start projects or activities. Larson (2000) defined initiative as "the ability to be motivated from within to direct attention and effort toward a challenging goal" (p. 170). This concept is congruent with Erikson's (1950) sense of an inner and outer direction and purpose that begins in preadolescence and helps facilitate all phases of life. The definition is broadened by Brandtstädter and Rothermund's (2002) contention that initiative not only involves *assimilative action* toward a goal, but also *accommodative action* to modify goals given new information.

The idea that initiative may also require accommodative actions gives it a place in Erikson's fifth stage of identity development. As young people seek to answer the questions "Who am I?" and "What is my place is society?" they also decide which interests propel them to action and how to accommodate for others' perspectives, errors in judgment, goal changes, or new opportunities. Accommodative action is important in a democracy as people develop empathy toward others and learn to help where needed (Barber, 1992).

A broader definition of initiative is particularly helpful in understanding how initiative is nurtured as young people overcome obstacles and challenges, learn from mistakes, and weigh choices. This aspect of initiative moves beyond psychosocial theory to cognitive development. In fact, Dewey (1938) posited the cognitive aspect of initiative when he discussed the meaning of *purpose*. "The formation of purposes and the organization of means to execute them," he claimed, "are the work of intelligence" (p. 62).

Albert Bandura (2001) contributed a focus on self-efficacy to the study of initiative when he included it as an essential component of agency. Self-efficacy is a belief in one's capability to accomplish goals that influence the events in one's life. According to Bandura (1994), self-efficacy beliefs are a determining factor in how we feel, think, behave, and motivate ourselves in the world. Bandura maintained that self-efficacy affected our thinking processes, how we were activated to action, and how we regulated our emotional states. People with high self-efficacy approached life and work with enthusiasm and as challenges to be mastered. Feelings of self-efficacy foster engagement.

Bandura (1994) believed that experience in "overcoming obstacles through perseverant effort" was essential to acquiring self-efficacy along with exposure to positive social models who exemplified sustained efforts to succeed (p. 2). Among the many factors correlated with civic engagement in young people, overcoming obstacles and exposure to civic role models are often found in the literature (Jennings & Niemi, 1981; Kahne & Sporte, 2008; Sears, 1975; Zukin et al., 2006).

Adolescents must make many choices, a key to developing self-efficacy (Bandura, 1994). As adolescents confronted what Erikson (1950) called *role confusion*, they chose activities that cultivated important competencies and social networks that supported their interests. Bandura argued that if adolescents were insulated from making their own choices during this period, they did not learn to navigate through problems, a necessary ingredient of initiative and self-efficacy.

Initiative involves the capacity to make things happen through action or *agency*. Agency, according to social cognitive theory, consists of a belief system and self-regulatory abilities to act. The four core features of agency are intentionality, forethought, self-reactiveness, and self-reflectiveness (Bandura, 2001). Of these, self-reflectiveness has been consistently correlated with civically-engaged young people (Andolina, Jenkins, Zukin, & Keeter, 2003; Colby & Sullivan, 2009, Winter; Kahne & Sporte, 2008; Wuthnow, 1995; Youniss & Yates, 1997, 1999; Zukin et al., 2006). The ability to reflect on action helped young people evaluate motives, pursue deeper understanding, address conflicts, and choose future civic actions.

A BLENDING OF THEORIES

Although Bandura's (2001) thinking relies on a social cognitive model of understanding, and Erikson's (1950) on a psychosocial model, the two share important commonalities. First, Bandura and Erikson both affirmed that initiative affects every aspect of development, transformation, and change. Bandura viewed Erikson's stage of identity development as an important time for the development of self-efficacy. While Erikson introduced the idea of initiative development in preadolescence, he maintained that initiative continued to develop in other stages. Adding the cognitive focus to Erikson's thinking expands them to encompass how our thoughts, like self-reflectiveness, affect agentic behavior.

Social cognitive theory takes the idea of human agency beyond Erikson's (1950) focus on individual development to understanding agency at the collective level, a hallmark of civic engagement and democratic processes. Collective agency represents the power we have to achieve through social interaction. People's shared sense of efficacy in their collective power has the potential to produce valued results. In fact, research shows groups that experience collective efficacy withstand setbacks and achieve higher performance (Bandura,

2001). Studies maintain the importance of collective agency, peer support, and social relatedness to youth civic engagement (Youniss & Yates, 1997; Zukin et al., 2006).

Other theories emphasize motivation rather than cognition in the development of initiative. Deci and Ryan (1985) wrote about the *energization* of development, the intrinsic motivation and self-determination necessary to initiate action. They posited that environmental factors during the years from early childhood through adolescence played a vital role in the development of intrinsic motivation. For example, they described *controlling* environments as detrimental to the energization process. In controlled environments children are pressured to think, feel, or behave in specific ways, or are rewarded only when they performed well. In contrast, *informational* environments provided acceptance based on children's existence rather than on behavior, urging them to make choices and think for themselves.

A controlling home often emphasizes academic achievement. Civic engagement is negatively related to the degree of control at home (Kahne & Sporte, 2008). Informational environments that provide opportunities for open social/political discussions are associated with engagement (Andolina et al., 2003; Colby & Sullivan, 2009, Winter; Kahne & Sporte, 2008; Wuthnow, 1995; Youniss & Yates, 1997, 1999; Zukin et al., 2006). The studies on college resume padding bolster Deci and Ryan's (1985) theory, suggesting when youth feel pressured to perform community service for the reward of college admission, they may be less likely to internalize the energy for sustained action over time (Davila & Mora, 2007; Friedland & Morimoto, 2005). When teenagers are rewarded by outcomes only, such as grades, high performance, or college acceptances, Deci and Ryan (1985) suggested they became dependent on similar outcomes to motivate them throughout life. Instead, if they are rewarded when they initiate new projects, explore new ways of thinking, or reach out to those in need, they develop patterns of intrinsic motivation that support future independent actions throughout life.

Mihaly Csikszentmihalyi (1997) theorized that if individuals did not learn to take charge of life's direction, they became controlled by external rather than internal forces. In his book, *Finding Flow: The Psychology of Engagement with Everyday Life*, (Csikszentmihalyi, 1997) the word *initiative* was used only once, but the psychic energy he described is quite similar to Deci and Ryan's (1985) description of the organismic energy that sparked intrinsic motivation.

Csikszentmihalyi (1997) introduced the word *autotelic*, defined from its two Greek roots: *auto* (self) and *telos* (goal). He portrayed an autotelic individual as one who is less motivated by external rewards and more motivated by internal flow. This type of person became involved in projects, overcame obstacles, and enjoyed problem-solving—characteristics of an engaged citizen.

Reminiscent of Csikszentmihalyi's work, Damon (2008) found that disengaged youth lacked a source of motivation he described as *purpose*. Both Damon and Csikszentmihalyi maintained that children thrive, develop competencies, and become engaged adults through participation in productive activities. Their work strengthens the position that initiative can be fostered through mastery experiences and through intentional support by adults who interact with young people. The civic engagement research also supports this thinking, not only showing the advantages of quality service experiences, but also the benefits of adult leaders who understand how to facilitate open dialog, nurture initiative, and maximize youth ownership in outcomes (Larson & Hansen, 2005).

Formal education is meant to prepare students to successfully master the adult world. However, research on the impact of schoolwork and homework on the development of initiative elicits concern. Data indicate that attending school and doing homework, accounting for an average of 25–30% of an adolescent's waking hours, offers limited potential for developing initiative (Larson, 2000). Although school-work provided high levels of concentration and challenge, it lacked a key ingredient of intrinsic motivation—an individual's capacity to choose desired activities.

This dilemma is highlighted by research that shows a pattern of concentration without the presence of intrinsic motivation during schoolwork (Csikszentmihalyi, Rathunde, & Whalen, 1993; Leone & Richards, 1989). Bandura (2001) reported that traditional class-rooms were not environments conducive to developing initiative or self-efficacy, and Damon (2008) showed that when activities were thrust upon children by external forces, disengagement resulted. Self-selected out-of-school volunteer activities and service-learning pro-grams may present richer opportunities for initiative development that lead to sustained civic commitment.

Studies from the 1990s and beyond show that young people who par-ticipate in specific types of learning environments outside of school are most likely to develop initiative (e.g., Csikszentmihalyi et al., 1993; Larson & Kleiber, 1993; Youniss et al., 1997). In one study of a youth activism program in Chicago, Larson (2000) found a rich envi-ronment for the development of initiative and agency, and that those agentic skills carried over into other aspects of the adolescent's life.

The data also showed that the program's structure and adult guidance provided essential components of the developmental experience. Other studies have demonstrated that experiences with a focus on specific civic issues, like homelessness or social inequality, are corre-lated with higher engagement, particularly when young people have the opportunity to discuss and reflect on their experiences (Davila & Mora, 2007; Kahne & Sporte, 2008; Youniss & Yates, 1999).

McLaughlin, Irby, and Langman (1994) studied youth in settings that had been structured to promote initiative. These organizations had numerous commonalities. First, although the original visions for the organizations came from adults, the direction and goals for the activities came from the youth participants. Youth held responsibility for setting goals, raising funds, solving problems, deciding schedules, and so on. These organizations all had real-world constraints that demanded challenge and complexity, and they all involved a commitment over time. Planning, practice, and rehearsal were essential components.

No comprehensive theory of initiative currently exists. It is clear that initiative is related to self-efficacy and the capacity for agency that has been described by Bandura (1994), and to intrinsic motivation as illustrated by Deci and Ryan (1985). Constructs like autotelic and flow (Csikszentmihalyi, 1997) and purpose (Damon, 2003, 2008) seem relevant, as does accommodation (Brandtstädter & Rothermund, 2002). Larson (2000) believed these concepts collectively provided a basis for belief that initiative may also be a key aspect of creativity, leadership, altruism, entrepreneurship, and civic engagement.

What are the key conditions required for initiative and intrinsic motivation to flourish? Larson (2000) believed that three situations need to exist. First, youth have to feel a deep, voluntary desire to be invested in an activity or experience. In other words, they have to have control over their choices of activities rather than be unduly influenced by parents or peers. Second, young people have to participate in these activities in real-world environments that contain rules, challenges, and complexities. Last, these voluntary activities must occur over an extended period of time. This condition ensures that activities include challenges and obstacles that need to be overcome rather than one-time events that demand little long-term commitment.

Larson argued that all three elements must be experienced together in order for initiative to be developed. Larson's concept of initiative drew from multiple disciplines and epistemologies, an approach that is likely to contribute to the research in valuable ways. Like others, Larson agreed that adolescence was a particularly good time to develop initiative, a period when young people acquired more formal operational reasoning and strategies for self-regulation.

PATHWAYS TO YOUTH CIVIC ENGAGEMENT

Scholars working in the area of youth development agree that engagement is a key goal of education and organized youth activities. This engagement must produce outcomes that challenge and motivate young people to be successful as well as active participants in their own development. Engagement creates habits of heart and mind that propel young people to dig deeper, try new approaches, ask questions, and learn from experience.

Researchers in youth civic engagement want to understand what encourages participation in the civic and political life of the nation. However, they often ignore the systemic relationship between engagement and citizenship, between individual development and civic involvement.

To exhibit sustained initiative toward the collective good, a person must also develop the individual disposition for action, including the capacities of agency, self-efficacy, intrinsic motivation, and self-regulation. It is this systemic approach that characterizes my research. Several important and recent studies in the field provide foundational support for this approach:

1. Study of Identity Development

James Youniss, an avid researcher in the study of youth moral development and civic engagement, has been involved in many studies that link individual development to collective civic action (e.g., Yates & Youniss, 1996; Youniss & Yates, 1997). Most of his research focuses on how specific programs or service-learning experiences increase youth engagement.

For example, Youniss and Yates (1999) described a 1997 case study in a predominately Black, urban high school in Washington, DC. The study explored how youth who served at a soup kitchen as part of a course on social justice reflected on their role in society, learned how government was organized to use its powers, and internalized moral principles related to poverty and homelessness. During the course of study, more than half of the 160 students who participated did more than the required service hours, suggesting to Youniss and Yates that young people found the experience engaging. Students also articulated images of their future, envisioning their potential to affect policies, education, and programs.

In the process of evaluating results of the 1997 case study, Youniss and Yates (1999) were drawn to the literature on moral development, particularly to studies that showed the relationship between moral commitment, self-concept, and identity (Colby & Damon, 1992; Hart & Fegley, 1995). They argued that morality should be studied as a part of identity rather than as a separate psychological function and articulated a rationale for including community service in school curricula.

Drawing on Erikson's (1968) theory of identity development, Youniss and Yates suggested that activities related to a particular religious or political ideology may have lasting impact on an individual's ongoing political-moral relationship with society.

The service program that Youniss and Yates (1999) studied was also "designed to generate a sense of agency and commitment through direct contact with the phenomenon of homelessness" (p. 365). It required guided self-reflection within a religious and social justice framework. While the study provided some evidence that this type of service nurtured adolescent identity formation in the manner suggested by Erikson (1968), the impact of the program on civic agency is questionable.

There would likely be many reasons beyond a sense of engagement in the current activity why some young people participated beyond the required hours, including peer pressure, family background, resume-building, and other previous experiences. In addition, the course did not meet Bandura's (1994) requirement for developing self-efficacy, providing opportunities to overcome obstacles through persistent effort.

A follow-up to the study several years later seems required to test the strength of the commitment. Even then, it would be difficult to attribute the development of agency to a single service-learning program unless that experience became pivotal in the adolescent's life or a particular role model became highly influential.

Youniss and Yates' (1999) discussion of morality and its relationship to civic identity and engagement is an important one, particularly when viewed through the lens of Westheimer and Kahne's (2004) framework of citizenship. While the development of morally responsible and compassionate young people as typified in Youniss and Yates' (1999) case study is associated with identity development, the link between moral responsibility and participatory or justice-oriented citizens is unclear and requires additional study.

Althof and Berkowitz (2006) examined the inherent conflicts in educating for citizenship versus educating for character, concluding that both are essential to civil society. They also noted greater synthesis is emerging. For example, Berkowitz (2000) argued much like Westheimer and Kahne (2004) that democratic citizenship requires moral development; however, citizenship must reach beyond character education alone. For pathways to civic engagement to be better understood, studies must go beyond moral behavior to examine the agentic behavior specifically associated with participatory and justice-oriented citizenship.

2. Study of Initiative

Reed Larson (2000), researcher at the University of Illinois, pointed to a lack of relevant theory and research on how to get kids engaged, motivated, and to take charge of their lives. Much of his recent research focuses on initiative, how it is developed through structured youth activities, and how it is related to political socialization and civic engagement. Larson and Hansen (2005) argue that strategic thinking, a form of pragmatic reasoning, is an essential component of agency. Within today's complex human systems, young people must learn "means-end thinking" that considers individuals and groups with different motives and perspectives (p. 328).

In a case study involving a youth activism program in Chicago, Larson and Hansen observed a group of Hispanic and African American teens who had participated in the activism program for varying lengths of time, from less than a year to three years. During the period of study, participants carried out several projects and action campaigns aimed at promoting "educational justice and equal rights for youth" (p. 332).

In addition to observations and a questionnaire, Larson and Hansen (2005) conducted interviews to attain participant interpretations of program experiences. Transcripts of the interviews were analyzed for underlying patterns and themes using grounded theory. Several important outcomes were noted.

Youth reported a diverse range of challenges and obstacles as they went about their work. In overcoming these challenges, they reported a deeper understanding of human systems. Rather than learning about civic or political systems in a classroom like participants in Kahne and Sporte's (2008) study or reflecting on their experiences like the participants in Youniss and Yates' (1999) study, these young people gained real-world experience as they engaged together in collective civic action. That experience was at times frustrating and disappointing. This process is reminiscent of how Erikson (1950) described both the planning and fumbling involved in the development of initiative.

Not only did the youth in Larson and Hansen's (2005) study learn to conceptualize human systems, they also developed approaches to influence those systems. The researchers identified three modes of strategic thinking in the data: seeking strategic information, strategic communication, and sequential and contingent thinking.

They also reported that these cognitive skills transferred to other aspects of the students' lives, including schoolwork, influencing others, and re-envisioning plans for the future. The experiential and problem-solving nature of the program seemed highly related to what Bandura (1994) defined as a mastery experience, contributing to the development of agency.

In the same case study, Larson and Hansen (2005) explored how youth learned skills in strategic thinking and the role that adult leaders played in the program. More often than not, participants relayed their knowledge in narrative examples of lived experience. Their stories provided detail of what led to success or failure and how they might overcome obstacles in the future.

Larson and Hansen conceptualized the student's thinking through "a cycle of self-initiated action, feedback, and learning" (p. 341) that resembled theories of self-regulated learning (Zimmerman, 2001). While the young people viewed themselves as agents of their own learning, the adult advisors also played a vital role.

Adults provided intentional "scaffolding" that helped young people facilitate their various social action projects (Larson & Hansen, 2005, p. 342). They participated as collaborators, providing guidance and structure. Their leadership styles were flexible and situational, sometimes giving direction, suggesting modifications of work, sharing expertise, providing support, participating in decision-making, and helping integrate multiple tasks. When young people floundered, leaders helped them get back on track and refocus on outcomes.

Adults encouraged evaluation of project outcomes through debriefing sessions that were opportunities for a type of reflection-on-action as described by Schon (1983). While adults performed these supportive functions, they were intentional about keeping ownership of the outcomes with the youth and "cultivating a culture and community of social change and strategic thinking" (Larson & Hansen, 2005, p. 344).

Larson and Hansen's (2005) study contributed to understanding how the cognitive aspects of strategic thinking and initiative can be developed in a youth activism program. It is important to note that the program contained the core assumptions and goals inherent in Westheimer and Kahne's (2004) description of the justice-oriented citizen.

What the study failed to examine, however, were the intrinsic motivators of initiative, how youth came to support the particular mission of the program. What experiences, relationships, or ideologies led them to choose such an activism program during their adolescent years? Larson and Hansen (2005) have suggested that future studies focus on the challenges and obstacles that kids face when working toward a civic cause because they believe this is key to understanding initiative. How kids interpret and act on their experiences, they contend, is critical to agency.

3. Studies of Motivation and Purpose

Three important multidisciplinary studies provide foundations for studying exemplar young adult populations, each broadly related to the purpose of my study. Nathan Teske, a political scientist, interviewed adult political activists drawn from environmental, social justice, and pro-life groups (Teske, 1997a, 1997b). Anne Colby and William Damon, developmental psychologists, interviewed extraordinary adult leaders in an effort to understand why they were committed to social causes (Colby & Damon, 1992). And most recently, William Damon and colleagues at Stanford University studied the development of purpose in exemplary youth (Damon, 2008; Damon et al., 2003).

Teske (1997a) approached his interviews with 60 adult political activists as a form of conversation, using open-ended, but structured questions to gather in-depth narrative data. One of the main findings of his study was the discovery that participants described their journeys as a fusion of moral and self-concerns, providing rich references to both moral beliefs and self-interest. Consequently, Teske argued that moral motivation in political behavior is not solely rooted in self-interest or solely based on altruistic impulses. Instead, it is part of the identity-construction process as individuals seek concerns that are both morally relevant and self-regarding at the same time.

Three themes revealed the origins of participants' activism: personal crisis, moral discovery, and lifelong commitment (Teske, 1997b, p. 51). Sometimes the themes overlapped, but one tended to dominate the others. People told moral tales of involvement, revealing a "morally and politically charged view of the world" (p. 61). Some described an inner crisis, a struggle for life meaning or purpose. Others retold a shocking discovery in the external world that caused them to question their own worldview. Those who felt lifelong commitments traced the origins of their activism to childhood and adolescence, to stories of parents and critical experiences that instilled values such as a concern for others or a love of the natural environment.

For many in Teske's (1997b) study, activism was a way to construct a satisfying self, "to develop and to live according to concerns rooted in a sense of who they are and who they want to be" (p. 96). Activists spoke to the "character-developing power of political activism" (p. 77) supporting identity-construction themes found in other civic engagement studies (Damon et al., 2003; Pancer et al., 2007; Youniss, 2006; Youniss et al., 1997; Youniss & Yates, 1996, 1997, 1999). Teske's participants were all adult, but many referred to their childhood and adolescent period as being pivotal in their life. One of the limitations of Teske's study for understanding the roots of engagement in the formative years of adolescence is that adult retrospective accounts are often inaccurate and lack detail. Teske's focus was on the origins of activism as an identity construct rather than specific learning experiences that developed initiative toward activism.

Recognizing the importance of moral commitment and character to citizenship, Colby and Damon (1992) interviewed 23 adults who had made outstanding contributions to society. They found common developmental patterns such as the ability to overcome fears, challenges, and obstacles. While there were large differences in material wealth and position, these moral exemplars displayed similar persistence toward human goodness.

Unlike Teske (1997b), Colby and Damon (1992) found little evidence of self-interest in their interviewees. It is likely that Colby and Damon's (1992) exemplars would be of the highest caliber of personally responsible citizens as well as participatory and justice-oriented citizens as defined by Westheimer and Kahne (2004). All made significant contributions to civic and political processes, including the fight against poverty, civil rights, peace, and the environment.

The study concluded that great moral acts of kindness and caring spring from everyday acts of morality. Colby and Damon claimed that moral exemplars seemed to go through life with little conscious effort directed toward how they would act in different situations. There was little separation between their moral, personal, and professional lives. While an examination of the challenges and obstacles they faced were part of this study, the focus of inquiry was on the meaning they attributed to those challenges rather than how obstacles contributed to the development of new strategies and approaches to influencing change.

In recent years, William Damon has focused on the study of purpose development and its role in helping young people gain a clear vision of what they want to accomplish in life. Damon defined purpose as "a stable and generalized intention to accomplish something that is at once meaningful to the self and of consequence to the world beyond the self" (Damon, 2008, p. 33). Using interviews and surveys with purposeful and non-purposeful youth ages 12-22, his studies concluded that "purposefulness among young people is the exception rather than the rule" (p. 8).

While Damon did not link initiative and purpose in the same way as Erikson (1950), he found numerous experiences that suggested a relationship between them. For example, purpose was expressed in behavior that was sustained over a period of time and linked to a deeper motivation to be engaged, elements reminiscent of Larson's (2000) definition of initiative.

Damon (2008) found that political and societal issues were not frequent sources of purpose compared to dedication to family, career, academic achievement, religion, and sports. In fact, he found that today's young people "show very little interest in society beyond the tight circle of their family and immediate friends" (p. 55).

Damon suggested this finding raised "warning flags for the future of our democratic republic" (p. 58). Although his study of exemplary youth included some young people who had made outstanding contributions to civic causes, the focus of his study was much broader, including those who had started small businesses, excelled in the arts, and pursued dreams in the world of technology.

Damon's (2008) research broke new ground because it examined purpose in adolescence and the process by which young people gain meaning in life. It suggested that learning how to set goals, developing long-term plans, and self-reflection were key components of developing purpose, but did not specifically explore how civic learning experiences might build these skills.

As in other studies that used exemplar populations, the focus of Damon's study was on identity development rather than on the development of agency or initiative, although it is clear that these constructs are interwoven. His study confirmed the importance of gathering narrative data directly from adolescents and young adults, indicating their ability to clearly articulate ideas, reflect on past experiences, and project future goals.

ENVIRONMENTS THAT FOSTER ENGAGED CITIZENSHIP

The research on how young people become engaged citizens points to numerous interrelated psychological, social, and cognitive experiences. Learning environments that facilitate both civic identity and the initiative to act seemed critical to further understanding civically-engaged youth. If an educator is defined solely as a classroom teacher, then civic education becomes severely limited in scope. However, if education is viewed as the shared responsibility of many, its scope not only broadens, but demands a more systemic understanding of how youth develop into engaged participants in a democracy.

John Dewey (1938) affirmed that a "primary responsibility of educators is that they not only be aware of the general principle of the shaping of actual experience by environing conditions, but that they also recognize in the concrete what surroundings are conducive to having experiences that lead to growth" (p. 35). It is precisely this shaping of growth experiences in the formative years my research was designed to explore.

Scholars are divided on the importance of civic participation versus political participation. Some argue that the teaching of high moral values and experiences that instill a sense of civic identity in young people should be of high priority in schools and after-school programs (Youniss & Yates, 1996). Because the numbers of youth who volunteer in communities is high, others suggest there be greater emphasis on fostering youth political engagement (Zukin et al., 2006).

Despite a wide range of approaches and perceived priorities, there is common agreement that today's young people lack the specific skills to address public problems (Levine, 2007). Studies that examine how these skills are developed by diverse youth in multiple-contexts of lived experiences are rare in the existing literature.

Current research suggests that identity and initiative are processes that may be implicated in civic action. Of these, identity, including moral-political identity, has received considerably more attention in the literature than the construct of initiative. While the citizen exemplars in my study were also moral exemplars, my study shifted the focus from how young people learn to find purpose in life to the learning experiences that help them formulate and organize the means of executing their chosen purposes. It differs from studies of activism that often focus on why youth adopt certain causes or challenge traditional civic or political structures. While some citizen exemplars were also activists, my study explored the experiences that helped young people strategize to accomplish collective tasks, learn how to overcome challenges, and affect systemic change.

Although the importance of initiative has been acknowledged in the literature for some time, the study of its role in democratic problem-solving and collective civic action fills an important gap in the current research. No other study has selected participants based on a frame-work of citizenship, looking specifically at young people who self-identified as participatory or justice-oriented citizens.

If we are to encourage young people to become co-creators of democracy, it is important to understand the challenges and obstacles they encounter, how they construct meaning to their experiences, and how the process is supported by others in their social worlds.

Studies suggest that civic engagement is an important context for ini-tiative development. To date, case studies have been used to observe the effects of specific programs on initiative development (Hansen, Larson, & Dworkin, 2003; Larson & Hansen, 2005; Larson et al., 2005). Studies have not looked at broader populations of highly engaged youth who have participated in numerous programs and contexts. Will data from this broader population show similar or different results when compared to research from highly effective individual programs? The study presented in the following chapters tested results from previous evaluative case studies.

The goal of my research was to learn ways to help less-engaged young people become more actively involved in civic life. Its highly engaged population, identified by Damon (2008) as the lowest sub-group of purposeful adolescents in the U.S., has developed civic initiative for reasons not fully understood. My study contributed to our understanding of this population and tested Larson's (2000) thinking about the initiative development process. It provided evidence of how initiative develops through positive learning experiences and what effective adult leaders, peers, families, and educators do to support its development.

Larson and Walker (2010) used qualitative research methods and surveys to determine how positive development occurs in extra-curricular activities and community-based programs. Through grounded theory, they explored how adult advisers in 12 high-quality programs facilitate these developmental processes. While their research is focused on the adult dilemmas of practice and spans many types of after-school programs, my research focused on the challenges and obstacles of civic engagement from the perspective of the participating adolescent. These research projects complement each another and through later comparison may be helpful in identifying similarities and differences between adult and adolescent perspectives.

My research study analyzed the underlying themes of challenging experiences encountered by highly engaged youth during the course of their community service work and the impact of those experiences on developmental outcomes and social agency. It examined how adolescents used activities, life experiences, classroom learning, and relationships to develop the initiative and means-end thinking that considered varying perspectives.

This book explores the experiences and relationships that propel young people toward civic action and how their initiative was sparked by ideologies, social institutions, and leaders. The study that provides the book's foundation was the first to engage a diverse geographical, ethnic, and socioeconomic group of adolescents committed to social and environmental causes. It adds to the body of literature on how young people develop the initiative, abilities, and skills to problem solve and actively participate in civil society.

3

Why Stories Matter

To change our world, we need to change our stories. It has always been this way. Since the days of our earliest ancestors, our ability to tell, listen to and remember story has been our key skill and conduit for knowledge sharing, communication, expression and most importantly, survival.

— Jeff Leinaweaver, PhD, *Storytelling for Sustainability: Deepening the Case for Change*

Stories help us see the world in new and different ways, and move us toward action. At their most basic level, stories connect people's brains in ways that help them co-create new stories—stories that transform society over time. Stories touch us because they allow us to connect to other people's joy, pain, and varied life experiences.

For example, when we reflect on the Civil Rights Movement in America, most people do not think of impersonal timelines of events. Instead, they remember stories that moved them to look at racial issues through a different lens. We think about Rosa Parks, a working seamstress who refused to give up her seat on a bus to a White man. We remember Medgar Evers, a NAACP leader in the early 1960s, as he described a Black man lynched in a town square for answering back to a White woman. The dead man's bloodied clothes were left in public as a warning to other African Americans who might dare to behave in similar ways.

These stories of discrimination and hatred angered people then, just as different stories of racism anger people in the 21st century. While the Civil Rights Movement transformed American society in many ways, new stories continue to shape our democracy. In more recent times, the deaths of Michael Brown, Eric Garner, and Freddie Gray, and the stories of African American youth incarcerated in unequal proportions by the U.S. criminal justice system are reminders that the struggle for social justice is never ending.

Stories matter. For many, the most profound memory associated with the murder of nine Black parishioners at Charleston's Emanuel African Methodist Episcopal church in 2015 was one of forgiveness. It was a story of how people of faith—families of the victims—stood in a court of law and told the accused shooter they forgave him. For those who watched and listened as their stories unfolded, these acts of faith resonated with millions around the country. They helped many people see these murders in a different way—an individual act that represented a much bigger social issue.

These and other stories are calls to action for citizens to co-create a better future—a future that represents the ideals of justice, equality, and freedom for all. Today's youth will be tomorrow's change makers, and the power of story will determine how they shape the future of democracy.

STORYTELLING STIMULATES LEARNING

Neuroscience helps explain why storytelling stimulates rich inner learning and what we might learn from the life stories of young people who grew to become advocates for social and environmental change. Although stories are unscientific, often imprecise narratives of human thought, they help organize and integrate the neural networks of the brain (Oatley, 1992). A well-told story contains emotions, thoughts, conflicts and resolutions. Louis Cozolino, a clinical psychologist who applies neuroscience to how humans develop secure relationships, claims that stories are essential to brain development and learning (Cozolino, 2013).

There are two essential parts of a story that stimulate the brain, according to Cozolino. First, stories contain a series of events, grounded in a period of time. Second, there is an emotional component to stories that gives them meaning and significance. If part of fostering young people's pathways to civic engagement is about enabling them to find meaning from their service experiences, you can see how stories give youth the mental templates for self-reflection. When youth feel connected to a story, their neuro networks are stimulated. Adults help young people unravel their feelings through reflective conversations.

The philosophy of John Dewey (1916, 1938) not only contributed to how we think about education in a democracy but also how we frame an understanding of experience. He did not see an individual's experience in reductionist terms; rather, he viewed it as an ever-changing, constantly unfolding process created by personal, social, and cultural interaction. Dewey's way of thinking emphasized ordinary life stories and how those stories helped individuals solve problems both personally and collectively.

In his book, *Excellent Sheep: The Miseducation of the American Elite and the Way to a Meaningful Life*, former Yale professor William Deresiewicz (2014) blames today's schools for failing to instill the values that led prior generations of Americans to work toward the betterment of society. Like John Dewey, Deresiewicz convinces us that the goal of education should always be "to leverage learning as an agent of social change—the kind of objective that makes leadership and citizenship into something more than pretty words." To accomplish this objective, Deresiewicz says we cannot continue to lead students, like sheep, to follow prescribed pathways to material, academic, and self-success, while ignoring the stories of those around them.

Rather than the *sheep* that Deresiewicz describes in his book, my research shows how today's young people find meaning through stories that connect them to people different from themselves, and how they use these stories to co-create a better society. These, too, are stories that matter.

NARRATIVE RESEARCH

With an emphasis on the learning experiences that helped young people become civically-engaged, I turned again to John Dewey's thinking. Dewey's (1938) writings on the nature of experience provide a conceptual framework for many narrative researchers (Clandinin & Connelly, 2000). Narratives are stories about action, linking human experiences with learning and meaning-making.

As a research methodology, narrative inquiry is a process by which experience is better understood. It is a systemic method for examining, organizing, and expressing lived experiences, creating meaning by "noting the contributions that actions and events make to a particular outcome" (Polkinghorne, 1988, p. 6). By remembering stories, the individual creates a dialectic between the past, present, and future (Gergen, 1994).

This interaction produces meaning-making through the interpretation of subjective experience. As such, it evokes a social constructivist epistemology characterized by the view that scientific knowledge is constructed through social interaction and hence expressed by language. Narrative inquiry is particularly well-suited to studies that examine the subjective meaning of life experiences as told by individuals.

> In considering people as constructors of their life stories, [narrative] research takes a giant step away from parsing human experience into predefined "variables" and requires of the researcher an equally major shift in perspective and approach. Rather than forming hypotheses, the researcher frames questions for exploration; in place of measurement are the challenges of deeply listening to others; and instead of statistics are the ambiguities of thoughtful analysis of texts. (Josselson, Lieblich, & McAdams, 2002, p. 3)

My research drew upon the concept of a three-dimensional narrative inquiry space as described by Clandinin and Connelly (2000). Using Dewey's notions of interaction, continuity, and situation as they relate to experience, the researcher pays particular attention to interactions between the personal and social; continuity between past, present, and future; and how these experiences intersect with the situation, or place.

THE SELECTION PROCESS

The population of young people in my study had to be able to articulate their stories as participatory or justice-oriented citizens (see Chapter 2), recalling experiences from their formative adolescent years. I chose a population of 18- to 21-year-olds because of their abilities to reflect on experiences, articulate ideas, and project future goals (Damon, 2008; Larson, 2000).

This age period was also a time period when Marcia (1966) posited that the adolescent identity crisis was resolved and a long-term commitment to social and political action had emerged. Thus, my study participants were defined as civically engaged youth ages 18-21 who met the following criteria:

Participants were nominated for this study by adults familiar with their civic engagement activities. The selection criteria were as follows: (a) 18 to 21 years of age; (b) a minimum of a 3-year exemplary record of sustained civic engagement; (c) commitment to a collective social or environmental effort aimed at improving the lives of others in their own communities or around the world; and (d) tackled challenging goals and contributed to problem-solving in real-world situations. The goal was to find a diverse group of participants, including gender, ethnicity, geographic location, political affiliation, and family income levels.

Following nomination, students completed an initial 30-minute online questionnaire. The purpose of the questionnaire was to identity information-rich cases, a purposeful design technique typical of studies that depend upon deep understanding from exemplar participants (Patton, 2002).

The questionnaire also produced narrative text for analysis through several open-ended essay questions. Upon evaluation of the data collected, a final group of young adults were selected to participate in in-depth interviews. These participants were chosen for their abilities to match the selection criteria and to provide equal gender representation.

Ethnic, socio-economic, geographic, and other aspects of diversity were also considered in selecting participants for interviews. While narrative studies are typically small in size, using a "maximum variation sampling" turns a potential weakness into a strength by allowing common patterns to emerge from the variation while "capturing the core experiences and central, shared dimensions of a setting or phenomenon" (Patton, 2002, p. 235).

Using a network of educators and adult civic leaders across the U.S., nominations of young people who fit the study's criteria were solicited by email. Nominations were concluded when 44 surveys were completed and enough males and females were identified who provided information-rich cases. After balancing the interview group by gender, primary consideration was given to balancing the numbers who identified themselves as participatory or justice-oriented citizens in the questionnaire in order to compare themes that emerged from these two groups of citizens.

This identification process occurred by analyzing participant responses to a series of multiple-choice questions designed to determine kinds of citizens as adapted from Westheimer and Kahne's (2004) model of citizenship. Lastly, selection consideration was given to achieving a mix of ethnicity, geographic location, political preferences, and other background items identified through the questionnaire.

STUDENT BACKGROUNDS

A total of 88 young people, 29 males and 59 females, were nominated for the study. For a variety of reasons, some chose not to participate. The greatest deterrent to participation was a lack of time due to current school obligations. The final study consisted of 44 participants, 13 male and 31 female.

Those who nominated students were affiliated with five main groups. Sixteen nominators were civic leaders of both large and small nonprofit organizations, including Rotary, Key Club, Habitat for Humanity, Heifer International, and the American Red Cross. Sixteen nominators were university-level educators, either directors of campus civic-engagement programs or professors. Six nominators were high school educators and two were members of the clergy. Four participants were invited to participate by the researcher because they received a civic engagement award publicized in a U.S. newspaper. Prior to their invitation, the award- sponsoring organization was contacted to confirm the student's eligibility and recommend the participant for the study.

All 44 participants completed an online questionnaire that consisted of background information and four narrative questions. The 44 participants ranged in age from 18-21 years and represented 22 states. Thirteen grew up in the Midwest, 12 in the West, 12 in the Northeast, 6 in the Southeast, and 1 in the Southwest. Home towns were a rural-urban mix, from cities less than 2,000 in population to major metropolitan areas. Participants were enrolled in colleges in 22 states and one Canadian province, from small liberal arts colleges to large universities. Ethnic backgrounds included 33 Caucasian/White, 6 Asian, 3 Hispanic, and 2 African American/Black. Religious preferences included 22 Christian, 18 Atheist/Agnostic, 1 Jewish, 1 Buddhist, 1 Muslim/Islamic, and 1 Hindu.

Family income levels were known for 32 participants. Twelve either did not know the income level of their parents or preferred to keep it confidential. Of the 32 who reported family incomes, 3 grew up in households with incomes less than $25K, 7 between $25K-50K, 6 between $50K-75K, 3 between $75K-100K, and 13 over $100K. A total of 36 participants attended public high schools, 4 attended private religious schools, 3 attended private independent schools, and 1 was home schooled.

PROFILES OF ENGAGEMENT

All participants were civically engaged, indicating they participated in activities "aimed at achieving a public good . . . through direct hands-on work in cooperation with others" (Zukin et al., 2006, p. 51). Eighty-three percent were cognitively engaged, indicating they paid pretty close attention to current news and information and talked with family and friends about social and political issues (Zukin et al., 2006). Sixty-four percent were politically engaged, indicating they liked to participate in activities that had the intent or effect of influencing government action (Verba et al., 1995).

Participants represented a range of political preferences. Twelve identified as independent, 12 indicated no party affiliation, 11 identified as Democrat, and 9 as Republican. Fourteen indicated a liberal bias, 9 a moderate bias, and 3 a conservative bias. Eighteen claimed no liberal/conservative bias. The data showed that those with no party affiliation, no conservative/liberal bias, and independents were equally likely to be politically engaged as those who claimed a political preference. Eighty percent of Democrats and 77% of liberals indicated they were politically engaged, compared to 60% of Republicans and 57% of conservatives. Seventy percent of Independents were politically engaged.

The research was designed to study highly engaged young adults considered to be participatory or justice-oriented citizens as defined by Westheimer and Kahne (2004). While survey questions elicited this information, participants often fell between Westheimer and Kahne's categories of responsible, participatory, and justice-oriented.

Three participants were classified as responsible, 5 as responsible-participatory, 10 as participatory, 9 as participatory-justice, and 17 as justice-oriented. Participants who identified as responsible were not selected for interviews because this research was designed to study participatory and justice-oriented citizens.

When asked about future careers and volunteering, 27 participants indicated a desire to find a career in some type of public service job, including education, government agencies, or non-profit organizations. Seventeen participants planned careers outside of public service, including law, business, media, science, and medicine. Those who did not plan a public service career indicated they would continue volunteering and being engaged in a purposeful cause for the foreseeable future. Thirty-two of 44 participants reported that their life-career purpose developed as a result of their civic engagement activities.

A SENSE OF PURPOSE

Although the participants in this study were outstanding examples of civically-engaged youth, what struck me most about them was how normal and happy they seemed. Their personal challenges were similar to other youth, often recalling how they used to be shy, unconfident, or uniformed—what you would expect to hear from any adolescent. They liked popular music, sports, and hanging out with friends like others their age.

Their stories often reminded me of those of my own child and stepchildren, stories that took one turn or another based on a single important life experience. What was different; however, were their abilities to articulate what was most meaningful in their lives and how a sense of purpose motivated their actions in the world. And it was intriguing to note that their happiness directly related to what they did for others more than attaining pleasure for themselves.

Twenty-two of the 44 participants were selected to be interviewed after completing the questionnaire. Interview selection was based on finding an equal number of males and females and balancing as many other factors for diversity as possible. Participants who were not interviewed, but contributed survey data to the study are listed in the following table with age and most passionate cause. The narrative responses of these participants are sometimes quoted in the remainder of the book, often used to expand and validate remarks made by those interviewed.

Non-Interviewed Participant Causes

NAME	AGE	PASSIONATE CAUSE
Allison	21	Improving environment
Brenda	19	Bettering lives of children
Cassandra	21	Promoting environmental awareness
Chandra	21	Empowering Asian Americans
Elizabeth	21	Getting quality produce to urban areas
Erica	19	Helping victims of domestic abuse
Estella	19	Banning fur farms
Grace	21	Helping impoverished people
Hannah	21	Eradicating global poverty
Kelsey	21	Teaching children to be future leaders
Lauren	21	Protecting rights of refugees & immigrants
Luke	21	Working for immigrant issues
Mariah	19	Helping impoverished children
Morgan	21	Teaching compassion
Natalie	18	Ensuring equal rights for women
Nicole	21	Promoting fair trade
Paige	20	Alleviating poverty
Peter	20	Protecting family values
Sierra	18	Lowering carbon footprint
Susan	18	Promoting micro-financing & education
Vanessa	20	Tackling issues of poverty & education
Whitney	21	Eliminating human trafficking

Twenty-two participants, 11 females and 11 males, were interviewed for the study. The stories of interviewees, listed in alphabetical order by pseudonym, are briefly introduced in the following paragraphs.

Amar

Amar, age 21, majored in history and hoped to attend law school. Born in England of Panamanian Hindu parents, his family immigrated to the U.S. when he was a child. In high school, Amar participated in a few civic activities, "the things every high school student does to get into college." But in his freshman year of college, his notion of civic engagement was transformed when he went to New Orleans to help rebuild houses following Hurricane Katrina. It changed his "perspective on a lot of things about service and community involvement." Housing became an important issue to him, and as a college senior he now co-directed his university's service-learning project in New Orleans.

Ashley

Ashley, age 18, was passionate about a career in media and television. Raised by a single mom, she "did not have very many luxuries." Her dad was "addicted to crack cocaine and he is in prison." Ashley was engaged in numerous activities in high school, including Key Club, hospice work, and the local food bank. At the age of 15, she visited Nicaragua with a church group where she learned "there are people out there that are way worse off than me." In Nicaragua, she was shocked with the state of the environment, with trash being burned and "tons of smoke going everywhere." She is now devoted to educating people about recycling through the creative use of media.

Brook

Brook, age 20, majored in sociology and minored in Spanish and Social Justice Studies. She grew up in a large family where her aunts, uncles, cousins, and siblings provided immense support when her mother was diagnosed with cancer and died when Brook was in high school. At age 17, she participated in a cultural immersion program in Mexico and Guatemala focused on "hands-on active learning as opposed to just sitting in the classroom." Her experience volunteering in a nursery in the slums of Guatemala City inspired her passion for public education, particularly for underserved populations. She helped found a chapter of Oxfam America on her college campus and continued as a leader in that program.

Byron

Byron, age 18, pursued a degree in information technology. Born in Germany, he grew up in the American South where he was active in Junior ROTC in high school. He enjoyed projects like canned food drives, adopt-a-family programs, and roadside cleanups—"stuff where you actually see improvement." Initially motivated to build a resume to get into the Navy Seals, he changed his mind about a military future. He began to find volunteer service extremely rewarding, particularly the camaraderie of working with others. Byron led numerous service projects and large-scale volunteer events. He was passionate about collective efforts to help his entire community, "not just those less fortunate."

Carlos

Carlos, age 20, began college as a biochemistry major. Of Hispanic descent, he lived half his life in Colombia and half in the U.S. in a single-parent family. His high school required community service and he participated in food drives, worked with autistic children, and raised funds for families in need. He was also the president of several service clubs. In his freshman year of college, he went to Guatemala on a service-learning trip where his life was forever changed. Reflecting on his own experience of growing up poor, when he went to Guatemala, he "was able to see how people survive with barely . . . barely anything." He returned to college, changed his major to civic engagement, and hoped to work for the UN.

Christina

Christina, age 20, majored in human resource management and minored in Spanish and Peace and Conflict Studies. Actively involved in her diverse urban high school and her Orthodox Christian church, she volunteered through Habitat for Humanity, Special

Olympics, and many other local programs. A few days after starting college, her boyfriend was killed in a car accident. After suffering from depression for a year, she realized with the support of her priest that "being low isn't going to help me and isn't going to help anybody else." Following a summer in Mexico working with orphaned boys, she now dreamt of running her own NGO that helped raise children out of poverty.

Danielle

Danielle, age 21, planned a career in agro-ecology or conservation biology. Raised and homeschooled in Mississippi with her two brothers, she married at 18. Her husband was in the Air Force and she attended college in Alaska, his first duty assignment. The daughter of a preacher, Danielle's father was her role model. She learned compassion first-hand as she accompanied him to nursing homes, funerals, and hospitals. It was not until she attended college, though, that she began to change the way she saw service from "something you did on the side when you had time" to "a lifestyle." A service-learning project with Heifer International ignited Danielle's passion for citizenship and environmental stewardship.

Ethan

Ethan, age 20, was interested in government and public policy. Raised in a conservative Jewish household, his Hungarian parents immigrated to America in the late 1950s. Particularly proud of his heritage, Ethan felt strongly about immigration reform. Although he struggled with learning differences and anxiety, he always enjoyed behind-the-scenes workings of government. He was inspired to work for the John Edwards campaign in high school and was involved in fundraising, phone banks, and Get-Out-the-Vote efforts. He was a passionate writer and student of history who had "not really found my 'one cause,' but I like to learn about and participate in a variety of causes . . . that improve people's lives."

Giovanni

Giovanni, age 21, was an Italian American majoring in English and sociology. He grew up in "an extremely wealthy family, extremely conservative." He attended a Jesuit high school and college where he participated in numerous service-learning experiences, including tutoring kids with disabilities, working in soup kitchens, and visiting homeless shelters. This work transformed Giovanni and he adopted much more liberal views than those of his parents. He developed "a thirst to be involved with people who aren't necessarily like me." Upon graduation, Giovanni planned to live in Burma where he anticipated teaching English and computer skills at a Jesuit school. He hoped to become a priest.

Jacqueline

Jacqueline, age 21, was a political science major and student body vice president of a large university. The daughter of Polish and German immigrants, her father and brother served in the U.S. military. Student council, speech, and debate were activities that fueled her passion in high school when she was drawn to the Republican Party through Barry Goldwater's philosophy in *The Conscience of a Conservative*. She was inspired by politicians like George Bush and Sarah Palin, has worked in many political campaigns, and interned at her State House of Representatives. Jacqueline had a deep interest in education and child welfare. Believing "that government is the very founding of how our society functions," she planned a career in public service upon graduation from law school.

Jared

Jared, age 20, majored in geography and was involved with an improvisation comedy troupe at his college. In high school, he served on the board of a community youth program where he facilitated conversations on alcohol and drug usage with other teens. He also served on student council. In his junior year, a service-learning trip to work in a Russian orphanage changed his worldview profoundly. It was "one of those experiences where . . . I was still processing it a year later . . . I'm still processing it now." Jared's experiences caused him to care deeply about homelessness. In college, he discovered a love for radio journalism and recently produced a story about rural homelessness in America.

Jennifer

Jennifer, age 19, was interested in economics, political science, and gender studies. Her long record of service and student government activities in high school "challenged me to engage outside my comfort zone and taught me how to work with others." As a junior and senior, she participated in an ambitious service-learning project to build an elementary school in Cambodia. This work was transformative for Jennifer and ignited a passion "about ending sex trafficking and violence against women," particularly in underdeveloped nations. She spoke to the UN about her school project and recently had the honor of introducing her role model, Nobel Laureate Nicholas Kristof, as he spoke about his book, *Half the Sky*.

Kaitlyn

Kaitlyn, age 20, created a major in International Social Justice. Emerging from being "very shy . . . in middle school," the list of her high school student government and community service achievements was substantial. There was one project, though, that gave her purpose—raising funds to build two schools in Kenya. Kaitlyn not only became a successful fundraiser, but broadened her perspective about human rights. She expanded that interest on a trip to Germany and Poland as a college freshman where she studied the Holocaust. Making the connection between different types of genocide, she furthered her commitment to "human rights in Africa, especially with educational policies and child soldiers."

Melinda

Melinda, age 18, was interested in the anthropological and cultural aspects of international development. After doing "required" community service work in high school, she began volunteering in her junior year with Amigos de las Américas, a non-profit NGO that trained and sent youth from the U.S. to live and work in Latin America. She spent two summers volunteering in Honduras, Nicaragua, and El Salvador where she "learned to be resourceful, resilient, and above all, a leader." She was "very passionate about immigration issues" and planned to pursue a career where she could make a difference in the lives of "disadvantaged peoples and with people who are in hard situations."

Michael

Michael, age 21, was a business major who also directed the homelessness projects at his university. A highly committed young man today, he was only marginally involved in community service in high school and "did not understand its importance." He was too shy to get involved in the large, highly structured community service club in high school and "didn't have the grades to be part of the Honor Society." He "just kind of fell through the cracks." When the opportunity in college arose to build homes in New Orleans, Michael decided to participate. "It was amazing . . . like eye-opening experiences." He doesn't yet know how, but hoped to combine business with his passion for homelessness.

Rasheeda

Rasheeda, age 21, majored in sociology and planned to go to dental school. Born in Kabul, Afghanistan, her Muslim family immigrated to the U.S. when she was a child. In high school, she volunteered hundreds of hours to tutor elementary school children and developed a passion for educational initiatives. At 17, she attended a global summit hosted by Mercy Corp that was a "very life-changing experience." Since then she has worked on behalf of many global issues, including HIV/AIDS, poverty, and access to education for women and children in underdeveloped nations. Rasheeda spoke before the UN twice, founded a college club for global advocacy, and was a successful fundraiser for her causes.

Ryan

Ryan, age 19, was exploring sociology as a major and loved to write and perform poetry and rap songs. His Asian American background and identity played a major role in his civic engagement experience, volunteering in Chinatown through most of his high school years. He led gambling addiction awareness seminars to Asian youth, facilitated writing/performance workshops for high school students, and hosted youth-run radio programs that brought attention to social issues. Ryan had a passion for empowering Asian youth and changing "the stereotype that Asian American teens are quiet and submissive." He attributed his success to learning "how to think" not "what to think."

Samira

Samira, age 18, loved astrophysics and philosophy. Born in China, her family moved to Singapore when she was 5, then to the U.S. when she was 10. The oldest child in a very traditional Chinese family, Samira "started feeling slighted" when her brother was born because her culture "favors boys." In high school, she participated in student government, a variety of service clubs, and political campaigns. As a senior, she participated in a year-long project focused on gender discrimination, where she studied, questioned, and tried to understand the issue with greater perspective. While she was still finding her own voice as a college freshman, Samira hoped to give voice to all women who felt undervalued.

Sarah

Sarah, age 21, majored in international development and social change. She had a long list of civic activities in high school, including student council, American Red Cross, and The Salvation Army. "The first moment I decided to get really involved in civic engagement" was on a three-week service trip to Costa Rica in her sophomore year. She returned and became a leader in a group that made clay mugs and sold them to increase awareness about fair trade. Sarah was "most passionate about making poverty history." In college, she joined the fight against poverty and disease in Africa through the One Campaign, an international advocacy group. She now served as one of its regional volunteer directors.

Scott

Scott, age 20, was a mass communication major with a keen interest in film and TV production. Describing himself as a "very shy, very quiet" African American from a modest background in North Carolina, Scott "didn't really care about getting involved in the community" as a teen. But in ninth grade, he began working with an anti-tobacco campaign that promised him a small stipend, travel, and job skills. "Challenged . . . and taken out of my comfort zone," Scott became passionate about ending tobacco usage. He regularly spoke to teens nationwide and lobbied before Congress for FDA regulation. His anti-tobacco campaign had been featured on NBC News and recently earned him a $100,000 grant.

Travis

Travis, age 21, majored in sociology and considered the Peace Corp as a next step in his career. He was a student government leader throughout high school and volunteered at an organic farm where he learned "how working literally in the dirt helped me to hone a will that has since been ready to tackle problems with the force of my own resources and means." The documentary, An Inconvenient Truth, was "a big thing that made me think about the environment" and inspired him to get involved with the Sustainability Office at his college. Working with renewable technologies in Nicaragua taught Travis "an incredible amount about myself" and "helped develop skills that I will use the rest of my life."

Victor

Victor, age 19, was a biochemistry and neuroscience major who planned to become an MD. He had a distinguished list of service activities in high school, including serving as Key Club International President. On a service trip to Uganda, he visited a site where his club raised funds to build a school. When a young African boy said he wanted to grow up to be an aeronautical engineer, Victor thought "it was just incredible to realize that this kid has this dream of making things that fly up in the air and he didn't even have a primary school." Since then, Victor devoted himself to making those dreams come true through leadership in an organization that worked to provide educational infrastructure in sub-Saharan Africa.

LISTENING FOR MEANING

As I conducted in-depth interviews with the young people listed above, I used questions that reflected the use of the three-dimensional narrative inquiry space as described by Clandinin and Connelly (2000). The semi-structured interview format contained questions that encouraged students to reflect on their experiences as active citizens.

The literature in Chapter 2 helped develop the themes for my questioning, but I also included open-ended questions that allowed the emergence of new and surprising data. Engaging the temporal dimension of narrative inquiry, I prompted students to ascribe meaning to their experiences retrospectively as well as how they envisioned their futures as active citizens. Engaging the inward and outward dimension of story, I prompted participants to talk about their inner feelings and motivations as well as the outward experiences that contributed to their development of initiative and associated skills of problem-solving, accommodation, and strategic thinking.

Engaging the dimension of place, I prompted for stories that described where learning took place, including organized programs, classroom experiences, student government, volunteer opportunities, church projects, and family experiences.

Upon completion of each interview, I wrote notes as a way of capturing my own experience of the interview, the participant, and any interpretations I had regarding the stories told. Clandinin and Connelly (2000) emphasized the importance of field notes in the narrative inquiry process. In Chapter 5, I share many of those observations, weaving them with the stories I heard from the students I interviewed.

INTERPRETING STORIES

While stories and storytelling are the major focus of all narrative researchers, the methods, approaches, and strategies used to interpret the lived experiences of participants vary widely (Lieblich, Tuval-Mashiach, & Zilber, 1998). My study used a hermeneutic approach to interpretation, a qualitative method of analyzing the content of textual data. A detailed account of my interpretative process can be found in my original study, *Civic Learning at the Edge: Transformative Stories of Highly Engaged Youth* (Price-Mitchell, 2010.)

Coding is a term researchers use to break data into themes and make interpretations. Coding is a "circular procedure that involves careful reading, suggesting categories, sorting the subtext into categories, generating ideas for additional categories or for refinement of the existing ones" (Lieblich et al., 1998, p. 113).

My coding was very comprehensive. In addition to breaking young people's stories into relevant themes, I queried the data for word frequencies and beliefs. I then applied matrix coding to the data, comparing themes between interviewed and non-interviewed participants and looking for relationships between themes and various participant attributes. Matrix coding queries enabled me to compare a wide variety of information and display results in tables that showed potential relationships.

For example, I compared how interviewed and non-interviewed participants described the attributes of their adult mentors and civic role models. I compared meaning-making by gender to note differences and similarities. And I compared intellectual, interpersonal, and intrapersonal challenges of civic engagement to explore differences by gender, citizen type, and other attributes. In total, more than 30 matrix coding queries were performed on the data.

When interpreting other people's stories, the researcher's relational role distinguishes itself from the more traditional objective role defined by positivist approaches (Pinnegar & Daynes, 2007). "Narrative inquirers recognize that the researcher and the researched in a particular study are in relationship with each other and that both parties will learn and change in the encounter" (p. 9). With this understanding, participants and researcher bring together their histories and worldviews as they are engaged in dynamic, changing relationships. The end product combines participant life experiences with those of the interpretive researcher in the form of a collaborative narrative (Clandinin & Connelly, 2000).

Not only did I see my role as the primary data collector and interpreter, I also recognized that my own story played a role in the research process. Many would view me as an exemplary adult citizen with a high degree of initiative. While I brought a number of biases based on my own life experiences, I also believe those same experiences made useful and positive contributions to the research.

My understanding of citizenship, human systems, and collaborative problem-solving processes enhanced my awareness and sensitivity to others' experiences in active citizen roles. My goal was to be cognizant of the impact of myself as researcher, placing my story in the background of the research. At the same time, I foregrounded the stories of participants in the research findings, allowing them to speak with honesty and authenticity to the reader.

Several procedures were used to validate whether the findings of this study were accurately conveyed from the viewpoints of the participants, adult nominators, and researcher. The first process involved triangulation from several sources of data, a way of validation that is common in qualitative research (Creswell, 2003; Robson, 2002). Information from several open-ended questions collected in questionnaires by all nominated participants was coded for thematic content. The content from the questionnaires was compared for similarities and differences with the narrative stories of interviewed participants. Triangulation validated that the themes found in the brief questionnaire responses were also found in greater depth and detail in those who were interviewed.

Creswell (2003) suggested several other strategies for validation that were employed in this study. In reporting results, I used rich, thick descriptions that sought to "transport readers to the setting and give the discussion an element of shared experiences" (p. 196). I also presented discrepant information, stories that conflicted with one another or brought out different perspectives. At all times, I attempted to clarify my biases as a researcher, reflecting in an open and honest manner about my processes of interpretation.

4

Voices for Change

Never doubt that a small group of thoughtful, committed, citizens can change the world. Indeed, it is the only thing that ever has.

— Margaret Mead

The young people who participated in my research study were introduced in Chapter 3, including their diverse backgrounds, civic interests, and engagement profiles. They are young citizens who are changing the world through a wide variety of social and environmental efforts. This chapter brings their voices to life in thematic ways, providing insights that sought to answer two questions: (1) How do civically-engaged youth describe the challenges they encountered as they worked for social and environmental causes? (2) How do they learn from others, construct meaning, and act to confront those challenges in ways that foster continued engagement?

This chapter introduces five main themes that emerged from my research. The initial sections, "Civic Engagement is Challenging" and "Heartfelt Connections Matter Most" address the first question. They focus on the major challenges faced by young people as they engaged in civic activities, exploring critical internal dilemmas in greater depth. The last sections address themes from the second question.

In contrast to the more in-depth storytelling found in the next two chapters, this chapter provides brief reflections in young people's own voices. These reflections, when categorized into common themes, give powerful insights into how young Americans find meaning and purpose through community service. There are wonderful nuggets of wisdom found in their own words.

CIVIC ENGAGEMENT IS CHALLENGING

The first of five main areas of findings, this section reviews three types of challenges described by participants as they took on projects in their communities and beyond. *Intellectual challenges* called for critical thinking, including confronting different worldviews, planning and organizing, and evaluating results. *Interpersonal challenges* engaged participants' capacities to interact with others, including attempts to motivate others toward service, dealing with leadership and power struggles, and facing difficult communication problems. *Intrapersonal* challenges compelled youth to look inward, facing emotional trials that pushed them out of their comfort zones, forced them to define their civic identities, and challenged them to deal with moral dilemmas.

Intellectual Challenges

Most young people shared intellectual challenges that involved problem solving and critical thinking. Intellectual challenges and obstacles fell into three main categories:

1. Responding to opposing worldviews
2. Planning and organizing

3. Analyzing and evaluating

Students seemed to welcome challenges and talked about the skills they gained as a result. Tasks that once seemed difficult in high school were viewed by college students as small in comparison to what they currently faced, indicating significant gains in intellectual development.

Most young people reported being challenged in face-to-face encounters with people who opposed their views.

> I had to explain myself . . . and challenge anybody who didn't agree with me. And at times it becomes frustrating because not everybody . . . stands on the same page. –Rasheeda

> The [program] coordinator always tried to ingrain in us, or encourage us to protest and go out to rallies and stuff like that. And he was like . . . "You should demand what is right." But I started thinking about what they were doing was not really teaching us how to think, but what to think. . . . What if some of the members do not agree with that viewpoint? –Ryan

> I personally like the UN and I think it's a good organization. And there are a lot of Jews who don't like the UN and think it's a terrible organization that only serves the detriment of society. . . . And that's something I do find currently difficult, especially when we have this very controversial [issue]. –Ethan

Some students discussed the challenges of planning and organizing in relation to their civic activities.

> What was challenging was this one event . . . had a lack of planning nearing the end. And I ran into quite a few problems. –Byron

> Every month has a challenge, so it's a lot of recruiting new members, and that's a lot of organizing and planning and working through administration at school to get things set up. –Sarah

The challenge was not having enough time to do my homework and sometimes not having time to spend with my family. –Carlos

Some students discussed challenges related to analyzing and evaluating information, programs, or budgets. Much of this work seemed to occur when students had to justify program funding or follow procedures to get things accomplished.

So what I did was . . . I wrote a brief, listing all the main reasons why, and some of the sensible reasons why, I had adopted this plan. –Samira

We still don't have a budget, because we have to go through certain steps and procedures, and then have a trial period before they allow you to have a budget, which just makes holding any type of event on campus so much more difficult. –Sarah

It was difficult because we had limited funds. And so we had to figure out ways that we were actually going to be able to build a library and get books. –Melinda

Interpersonal Challenges

All young people talked about interpersonal challenges of working with or engaging others during civic activities. Three main interpersonal challenges were described:

1. Motivating others toward service
2. Leadership-relationship issues
3. Communication problems

Once participants were committed to a civic issue, they wanted others to feel their passion. This often resulted in frustration as they interacted to motivate friends and strangers to get involved. Most students provided examples of the challenge of motivating others to become engaged in service.

The biggest challenge was coming up with ideas to make it relate . . .

that they would actually care about it. . . . Unless you have an experience like me . . . in Nicaragua . . . you don't always think of it as relating to you. –Ashley

What gets you down a lot is people who say we can't do it. Like we don't have the time to do it. We don't have the funds to do it. We're too busy to do it. –Kaitlyn

I see that others aren't as passionate as I am. . . . I wish they would get more adamant for themselves. That's a huge problem, especially when the incentive is a scholarship or some kind of financial stipend. –Christina

Participants talked about the challenges of dealing with people on a personal level when working on collective activities. Because of their young ages, they were often new to leadership roles. Supervising or trying to direct peers was challenging as was being in leadership situations when others chose to break rules. More than half of students talked about this challenge.

I was working with a lot of teenagers that were pretty much my age, maybe a year or two younger. But the difference was that I was sort of their supervisor. . . . I found it challenging to establish myself as the project leader. –Ryan

A lot of the biggest challenges have nothing to do with service. On all [service-learning] trips, there is a strict "no alcohol" policy. . . . And as you can imagine, dealing with a bunch of college students, that rule was starting to get ignored. –Amar

Students often pointed out the challenge of communicating clearly and how difficult it was to communicate with large groups. For those who participated in foreign programs, language barriers also presented challenges to communication. A number of youth commented on this obstacle.

One of the biggest and most persistent [challenge] is communication.

There are a lot of people to coordinate communication between and the modes of communication aren't always reliable. –Danielle

There was a communication gap on a number of different levels. –Travis

I only had two years of Spanish so I could barely communicate with my [host] family. That was definitely a really big challenge. –Sarah

Emotional Challenges

All of the young people interviewed told stories of emotional challenges, the intrapersonal struggles that took place within themselves. Three main intrapersonal challenges were described:

1. Feeling out of emotional comfort-zones
2. Defining civic identities
3. Facing moral dilemmas

Almost all of the young people were self-reflective about their civic experiences, particularly of events and circumstances they depicted as life-changing. While many found their out-of-comfort-zone experiences transformative, they also coped with an array of uncomfortable feelings that were emotionally demanding. Circumstances that ignited these challenges included saying goodbye to children in foreign countries, interacting with people very different than themselves, experiencing poverty, being exposed to physical danger, and witnessing suffering. Most shared stories of these discomforts.

Honestly, when I first heard we were going to be going door-to-door [in New Orleans] I thought it was the most awkward situation that I'd ever heard of in my life. –Amar

So it turns out to be a very intense, focused experience, and then it's over, which is a challenge. –Jared

It was completely out of my comfort zone going halfway around the world to a third world country. . . . There are the language barriers . . . and the weather. Even the food, basic meals was a whole challenge . . . not to mention land mines. So it was scary going into it. –Jennifer

Most young people articulated the inner challenge of defining their civic identities, from seeing service as a collection of activities on a resume to seeing service as a way of life. The process of constructing a civic identity normally did not emerge from participating in any one civic experience or program, rather it appeared to be an ongoing process of self-discovery that lasted years and is still ongoing. Students spoke reflectively when talking about this challenge.

I think the hardest part was just changing the way I saw service myself. . . . it made me look inside myself for what my real motives were. –Danielle

I think motivation really comes from the open question of what it means to serve. –Travis

Another challenge is that I'm a business major. I have no idea how I'm going to make . . . service . . . a part of [business]. . . . It's like capitalism versus helping people. . . . And that's a big thing I've been struggling with this year. –Michael

Student stories contained many references to morality and difficult moral choices. Some questioned the value, on moral grounds, of service-learning programs that were more about volunteer experience than about the people served. Or they questioned programs that exposed students to orphaned children or poverty for just a few days. Others grappled with the best ways to help new friends in foreign countries that needed money. Many young people elaborated on these moral challenges.

I know I was just there with them for three days and since then I've had moral issues about how much time is okay to be in someone's life and help them and then just leave. –Brook

It was an experience . . . that breaks every rule that you are taught about service and especially international service in poor areas, that you don't give money because you don't want to create a dependency. And so it was a really, really emotional experience for us because he was our friend and we wanted to help him and we thought about all the resources in our lives. . . . And so it was a situation where we knew we could be of immense help but we couldn't be helpful. And, you know, I wouldn't say that this is something I've resolved. –Jennifer

We were building a house with Habitat for Humanity. . . . The site builder was putting . . . paint thinner . . . right into the ground. It was leading right into a lake about 100 yards from the house. . . . And it just seemed totally crazy to me . . . but I bit my tongue. . . . In large part I knew I was an outsider and knew there wasn't anything . . . I could do to change things. . . . It was a lot more [important to think about] preserving relationships. –Travis

In addition to making moral decisions and choices for themselves, half of those interviewed also questioned the moral choices of friends or family members.

It was kind of interesting because there were some people who were really moved by [the devastation in the Lower Ninth Ward], and other people who were just taking pictures of it. I thought that was wrong. It was very touristy. –Michael

As much as I can scorn my parents' wealth and [their] attitude, the fact is if they didn't have that wealth or that attitude of elitism, then they wouldn't have sent me to [a private high school] and I wouldn't have gotten the education that I did and I wouldn't be able to feel the way I feel. –Giovanni

The intellectual, interpersonal, and emotional challenges of civic engagement were described by all young people interviewed. These challenges not only seemed to play a significant role in defining civic identity for participants, but also in facilitating development of positive skills and abilities. Young people learned to solve problems, think critically about civic causes, interact with others, and reflect internally on their experiences and moral values. Because the emotional challenges of civic engagement seemed particularly poignant to students, these experiences are more fully explored in the next section. Later in the chapter, the developmental benefits of these challenging experiences are examined as well as the meaning-making that was constructed from them.

EMOTIONAL CONNECTION MATTERS MOST

Of the three types of challenges described by participants in the previous section—intellectual, interpersonal, and emotional—the intrapersonal challenges that pushed young people out of their emotional comfort zones were described as most transformative to developing civic purpose and identity. These were the experiences that connected young people's hearts with social causes that compelled them to take action. This section focuses on those critical emotional experiences that deepened participants' inner drive toward service, including adolescent out-of-comfort-zone experiences, childhood incidents, personal hardships, and other inspirational experiences.

Out-of-Comfort-Zone Experiences

All of the students interviewed discussed *out-of-comfort-zone* experiences as being key catalysts to their sustained civic engagement. Most often occurring between the ages of 15 and 19, these out-of-comfort-zone challenges remained a source of current inspiration and motivation. These experiences created emotional discomfort and pushed youth to see the world differently. In each situation, moral reasoning was required. Most youth talked about coming face to face with less privileged people as being extremely challenging, uncomfortable, and perspective-changing.

To go to such a poverty-stricken area for the first time . . . was a very huge eye-opener. . . . I just remember being so far out of my comfort zone. . . . It was a huge cultural shock. –Ashley

I've been to Philadelphia many times as a child . . . seeing homeless people all the time . . . being told by my parents to just keep walking. . . . Through a homeless outreach site at my school, [I walked] around just finding people that are homeless . . . talking to them, saying this is where you can get a shower . . . clean clothes or a permanent mailing address. . . . This other world is sort of open to you . . . talking to them you just find that they're really people just like you. –Giovanni

I don't mind being in front of people. But when you ask me to sing and dance in front of people, forget it! . . . The students I was dancing with weren't wearing shoes. . . . Many were missing teeth . . . because of decay. . . . But we were having fun together . . . and we were having this experience that I wouldn't have traded for anything. . . . That one experience [made me see] that I can actually do something for the world and I will. –Jennifer

Many youth talked about out-of-comfort-zone experiences unrelated to poverty that forced them to think or feel differently about others or a particular cause.

I saw so much suffering in the nursing home and people who are so painfully lonely . . . their needs hadn't been tended to. . . . It was frightening for me to go there for a long time. –Danielle

[We] watched different clips on how to handle bullying situations. . . . And then [the leader] would do experiments with each of us. . . . He came up to me . . . I was wearing a necklace. . . . He said, "I can strangle you with this. And if you got in a fight, someone might kill you just by grabbing and strangling you with this necklace." It really scared me enough to open up my eyes on what I can do [to work for violence prevention]. –Kaitlyn

It was a music video by Sarah McLaughlin . . . called World on Fire. . . . Once the lights were switched back . . . more than half of the room was in tears. And I was just first a little overwhelmed with all the information we had learned . . . in the last three days, and then to be shown this video . . . through the form of art and a visual—it added more to the emotional aspect of being human. So that definitely did turn on the switch. –Rasheeda

Childhood Memories

While not transformative at the time, half of the interviewed group of students also recalled uncomfortable and poignant stories from their childhoods that, upon reflection, may have helped shape their civic identities. These experiences were emotionally challenging and supported the general theme that young people grew and learned from these experiences, revisiting them at later stages of development.

> I remember . . . one incident in kindergarten . . . at lunch time [when] I brought in a sandwich that was . . . filled with Asian meat. . . . The kids were just like "Oh, Ryan is eating dog food. He's eating dog food." It kind of upset me then. . . . Now looking back, I can say that it was kind of a racist incident. . . . It was incidents like that that were kind of the catalysts for me to be involved in the community. –Ryan

> Here's a memory that sometimes I revisit. . . . I must have been six years old . . . and on a tee ball team. . . . I brought a [softball] to practice. . . . And I didn't really know the difference, but it was a little bit squishier, I guess. . . . And the coach picked it up and said, "Man, whose ball is this? This is like a woman's ball." . . . I was embarrassed that I'd brought a woman's ball to this really macho sort of gathering. . . . He threw the ball into the woods. . . . And so I think from a young age, I've been aware . . . that people influence each other and it has always made me feel like I can be, not even necessarily a good role model, but just like a positive presence. –Jared

Personal Hardships

Personal or family struggles provided motivation to help others who had suffered through similar experiences. In addition to relating specific transformative events in the above categories, some young people also spoke of family situations that fueled an interest in such causes as equal rights, gender discrimination, victim rights, hospice work, elderly care, and immigrant issues. Again, while these experiences were not the result of civic engagement challenges, they support other stories of emotionally challenging experiences that were transformative to civic learning.

> When I was nine years old my mother was in a very abusive relationship. . . . From that age on, I knew I was going to be a prosecutor. I knew I would be the one who helped victims and tried to pull them up when they were down. –Erica

> It's not very easy being an immigrant. . . . My mom is a single parent. . . . Sometimes we didn't see her because she was always working to either pay the rent, buy food . . . clothes . . . books. –Carlos

> When I finally put my tragedy into perspective, I realized . . . I can still help others. –Christina

Inspired by Others

While almost all young people spoke of transformative experiences as being those that pushed them out of their own emotional comfort zones, some young people also shared more comfortable, inspiring stories that deepened their motivation toward service. Many of these stories involved catching inspiration from other individuals, collective events, books, documentaries, or other media.

> It was nice to know that there were actually peers out there that wanted to get involved in these issues. And they had the passion to actually do something about it. . . . It was a very, very life-changing experience for me. –Rasheeda

> Just the blending of the different people coming together and uniting. And that we all felt the same way on the issues kind of inspired me. –Jacqueline

Everyone was very happy for us to be there. . . . I just remember thinking that if people had such hardship in their lives and they were still being so nice, you know, something pretty cool had to be happening there. –Michael

Emotional challenges and experiences were significant in all young people's civic engagement. By far, challenges that occurred during high school or freshman year of college that involved face-to-face encounters with human suffering were most transformative. These events pushed young people out of their emotional comfort zones to face moral dilemmas and see the world differently. Young people described these experiences as life-changing. Emotional experiences of other kinds, like memories from childhood, personal hardships, or events that inspired service deepened participant motivation to become engaged in their communities.

The sections of findings discussed above were primarily focused on addressing the first of two questions: "How do civically-engaged youth describe the challenges they encountered as they worked for social and environmental causes?" The second question, "How do they learn from others, construct meaning, and act to confront those challenges in ways that foster continued engagement?" is the focus of the next three sections.

ADULT SUPPORT IS ESSENTIAL

Adults played a significant supportive role in the lives of all interviewed young people. During my analysis, the metaphor of scaffolding emerged from participant stories. Like the scaffolding that supports workers who build or repair physical structures, study participants described a clear system of adult support without which they would not be the people they are today. Young people made a distinction between four types of scaffolding, each of which played an important role in how they developed. The four areas of support came from long-term adult mentors, civic role models, parents, and program leaders.

Long-Term Mentors

Young people made a clear distinction between adult mentors and the more inspirational role played by civic role models. These non-parent mentors emerged during high school and were most often educators. However, they were sometimes members of the clergy or older family members. The primary role of adult mentors was to help youth develop self-efficacy, or what young people often described as a belief in themselves. Mentors accomplished this through

1. Supporting and encouraging
2. Listening
3. Setting high expectations and pushing
4. Showing interest in youth as individuals separate from academics or civic activities
5. Fostering self-decision-making
6. Providing another perspective during problem-solving

It was common for students to be in regular touch with their high school adult mentors in college and for the mentor to be considered a valued friend.

All but one young person had relationships with one or two non-parent adult mentors that spanned two years or more. Each of the six mentor qualities listed above were cited by almost all of the students interviewed through stories that often mentioned several attributes. Rather than dissecting each attribute with supporting quotes, the following is a compelling and well-articulated chorus of comments that are representative examples of the combined qualities of adult mentors.

Getting support from somebody who isn't your parents is very touching. . . . She had no obligation to listen to me, and yet she still did. It gives you strength in a way that your parents . . . really can't give you. –Melinda

He encouraged me to keep writing, to channel my emotions into some form of media, rather than keeping them bottled inside of me and being upset about things. –Ryan

He helped me more with the "Jennifer" side of things, rather than . . . academics . . . or service, or what not. Even if I messed up something horribly . . . it would turn into talking about how I was doing as an individual. –Jennifer

He was really like my mentor, [we talked about] anything, even little things. –Giovanni

He was always there to help when I needed him. It wasn't him telling me what I should do . . . he was just there to keep me going which I thought was very important because I knew that I could pull stuff together. It's just nice having someone there all the time to let you know. –Byron

[He] helped me see the success of an event isn't just measured by one thing. . . . After everything started going not quite the way I had planned, [he was] able to step in and let me know that it was alright. –Victor

They were right alongside me. . . . And I could go to them and talk about anything, any difficulties. . . . I talked to them about everything. . . . It was like my possibilities were endless for whatever I wanted to do in the world. –Ashley

He wouldn't try to tell me what to do. . . . He would instead just be thoughtful and quiet and then he would remind me who I was. . . . he showed that he had faith in me and he knew that I would make a good choice. –Danielle

He was just really, really good about listening. . . . And the other teacher, who also became a friend of mine . . . she told me that if I ever needed help with anything then I could come to her too, and so I started doing that. –Brook

He's the one who continues to motivate me the most. . . . Also from a spiritual sense; he was the one who . . . put everything into perspective. –Christina

I would talk to her about what I wanted versus like maybe what my parents wanted. . . . our discussions centered around independence and what it meant to be an independent person and not rely on other people for validation. –Jared

I had two mentors in high school. . . . They helped me so much. I think basically everything I did was because of them. . . . They were always pushing me. –Carlos

[These two teachers] were supportive, which was what counted. –Ethan

You don't want to limit yourself. That's what she told me. . . . I really enjoyed talking to [this teacher] . . . just about life. . . . we were friends. –Samira

[She] pushed me to do more than I ever thought that I would. –Michael

So if I ever had a problem . . . I could run it by him. . . . he was just very reassuring. –Jacqueline

He's been very helpful for me in opening up my eyes . . . and helping me learn more about . . . how I can do it by myself and not rely on having to get [others] to help me. –Kaitlyn

I went to my assistant principal all the time. She was a very approachable person and . . . a very good friend of mine. And I still keep in contact. . . . She would always give me that encouragement and that influence that things will always be better. . . . She made me realize that if you really try hard . . . you can always go after what you dream. –Rasheeda

I learned a huge amount [from them]. . . . Not as much asking them for advice outright, but a lot by observing them. . . . I looked to them and to their guidance often. –Travis

She's always been the one to help me take a minute, breathe, and reassess the problem and find the solution. –Sarah

She didn't impose her beliefs on me. She just would lead me to my own answers. . . . I felt like I was talking to a friend who knew just a little more than me. –Scott

Amar, the only interviewee who did not have a non-parent mentor in high school, discussed the very close relationship he had with his parents, particularly his dad. He also indicated, because of a number of staff changes, his high school was not a stable place for him to find the same support and encouragement he found at home. Amar described qualities of his parents that were similar to the attributes other students assigned to adult mentors, including an ability to push him to stepping up for who he was.

Civic Role Models

All young people in this study described an adult they knew who most exemplified their idea of a civic role model and why. Civic role models were described in quite different terms than adult mentors, although for several, the same person served as both role model and mentor. The primary task of civic role models was *inspirational*. While adult mentors seemed to provide developmental scaffolding, the civic role model was a beacon at the top of the support structure. Civic role models were valued for the following:

1. Passion and ability to inspire
2. Clear set of values
3. Commitment to community
4. Selflessness
5. Ability to overcome obstacles

These attributes ranked in the order noted by interviewed and non-interviewed participants. The types of role models identified are shown in the following chart.

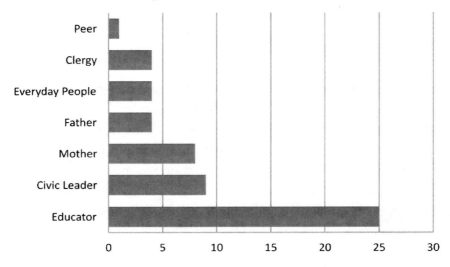

Regardless of the type of person described by participants, more than half of them mentioned at least one of the five attributes noted above, often in the same sentence or paragraph. The following participants provided representative examples of the five attributes of civic role models.

1. Passion and ability to inspire

It was their continued dedication to bettering the world—bettering their community, and then, in turn, bettering the world. The fact that . . . they could be making so much money with a college degree, but instead they're coming back working for a non-profit. Or teachers—the fact that they're so dedicated to teaching students and helping students and empowering students. . . . That's . . . such a meaningful gesture. . . . they're always trying to give back to the next generation. That really inspires me. –Ryan

2. Clear set of values

She has a clear sense of what is important to her, therefore she puts forth the effort to improve and create things that will make a difference. –Natalie

3. Commitment to community

She exemplifies my idea of a civic role model because she was active in the community. She attended city meetings and volunteered her time for a variety of projects. She was ambitious and charismatic; you could not help but love being around her. . . . [She] continues to be selfless and works for the benefit of others. –Allison

4. Selflessness

He never saw social barriers. He saw people's needs and he acted on them, no matter what background they had, no matter their circumstances. . . . He was never afraid to get his hands dirty. He was very politically aware and followed politics meticulously. He never made an uneducated choice in his voting and was always proud to support a campaign he believed in. [His] lifestyle was a type of service. His political action was a type of service. My father taught others to serve. –Danielle

5. Ability to overcome obstacles

In all my experiences, the individual who distinguishes himself as a true civic role model is not the person with the best job title, the most responsibility, or the greatest fame to his name. Instead, he is an incredibly hardworking individual who has faced unimaginable obstacles in his life, yet continues to persevere to support his family and encourage his community. . . . Vey survived the Cambodian genocide. . . . He earned his education in a system where those who succeed are the ones who bribe officials. He has dedicated his life to give back to his community. . . . Wow! What an individual . . . and the best civic role model. –Jennifer

The Role of Parents

Of the students interviewed, more than half mentioned the positive influence of their parents in relationship to their civic engagement, while only a third reported their parents were highly engaged themselves. Like adult mentors, parents provided emotional support and encouragement. However, their primary role was to scaffold moral development through instilling values. All young people referred to their family values as being foundational to the people they became. This theme was also reflected in participant surveys of those not interviewed. The rich descriptions below came from two interviewed and two non-interviewed participants.

> The philosophy that my parents embedded in my head is "don't ever stop doing something you love because of other people. Because if other people are the reason you're going to leave something, then obviously . . . your passion for that isn't as powerful as your hate for somebody else." –Christina

> I think first of my dad. Even though I only really realize it now, he has set an example for me of how to live in a moral way. –Amar

> My mother is the reason why I'm the woman I am today. She showed me that every bad situation life throws at you can be turned into a light at the end of a tunnel for someone else. –Erica

> I followed my own path for civic duty, but I looked to the strong examples that my parents set throughout their daily lives in order to stay true to the spirit of service and to not operate solely through a personal agenda of advancement. –Grace

Program and Institutional Leaders

This study did not evaluate specific civic programs or the positive or negative aspects of organizations, schools, or institutions. However, it was clear these groups played a significant role in fostering civic action. Most of the 44 participants in the study listed more than a dozen programs or organizations to which they had been affiliated since freshmen in high school. Transformative learning experiences occurred in all types of programs, from very small locally led efforts to projects in much larger organizations. While many programs were affiliated with schools, not one student described a transformative learning experience that occurred in a traditional classroom. Several described school courses designed around service-learning opportunities and performed in partnership with civic organizations. One interviewee provided a particularly rich description of such a class.

> The program he uses in his Geography 101 class is to introduce students to community service in a little bit different way that gets them involved in the actual community instead of just learning about it in the classroom. He uses an NGO, Heifer International, as a tool to accomplish that. The students are given a project where their goal is not to raise funds, but to raise awareness of Heifer International. And they are required to engage the community in some sort of face-to-face exchange. . . . At first, I was pretty skeptical . . . and a little irritated that I was being compelled to do service work. . . . As I was required to identify an audience and coordinate schedules and develop a mode of presentation that would be meaningful and hopefully encourage discussion and raise awareness, I began to see the long-term effects of what I could be doing. It had a very big impact on how I understood service. . . . Because once you've educated someone . . . about what they can be doing to help their community, what other communities need, they're going to take that with them throughout the rest of their life. –Danielle

Often, the challenges and obstacles that young people had to overcome directly related to organizational or program leadership or structure. Yet participants seemed to learn as much from programs where major problems were perceived than from those where they felt more comfortable. The decision to leave an organization was usually accomplished with a great deal of gratitude for what they had learned about themselves. Most students had the capacity to construct meaning from programs or leadership situations that were less than ideal.

> I ended up leaving that organization because I did not really agree with the way that they dealt with things or the way that they ran the program. . . . [But] my experiences . . . were very meaningful. –Ryan

I just try to turn the negative things into future opportunities. . . . I don't try to blame other people. . . . What happened is over with and okay, how can we learn from this? How can we make it better for next time? –Christina

Only a few students mentioned a strong faith in God as a significant motivator of civic engagement. But the positive impact of religious institutions and programs was mentioned by one-quarter of those interviewed. These programs and their leaders were instrumental to their initial volunteer experiences, transformative learning, and moral upbringings.

I was really involved in my church in high school . . . so a lot of [encouragement for volunteering] had to do with my upbringing. –Sarah

I think it was the first time I ever really saw helping others hands-on. And then at that point I got involved in my church to do the same thing. And then not only through branching out through the church . . . I started to branch out from my church. –Ashley

Being introduced to the Ten Commandments as a young person . . . became kind of the source of a set of open questions for me. –Travis

What was clear from young people's stories was a recognition that no matter what program or organization they became involved with, the most important initial and long-term program quality was whether they developed positive, empathy-based relationships, not only with fellow volunteers and program staff, but also with those they served.

I can't look at this list of the things that I did and think about something I didn't enjoy doing or that wasn't meaningful for me. And a lot of it has to do with the people I worked with. –Jennifer

I think that the personal relationship helps because when you feel connected with somebody then you're much more inclined to try to make their life better. –Melinda

And we all just got along really well. We all became really good friends, and we stayed friends since then. –Michael

The narrative data in this section described the system of adult support experienced by study participants. Most significant was the finding that all young people had long-term relationships with adult role models during high school that facilitated the development of self-efficacy. These mentors, mostly educators, were credited by young people as having a great influence on the people they became. Civic role models differed from adult mentors, providing mostly inspiration rather than direct coaching. Like adult mentors, parents provided support and encouragement and also instilled a clear set of moral values.

Civic program and institutional leaders afforded participants structured opportunities for engagement, including highly valued transformative experiences. Young people learned about themselves and civic causes in all types of organizations, even when experiences were not positive. The next two sections examine the developmental benefits of civic engagement as described by students, and what learning they constructed about themselves and the world around them.

GIVING BACK SPARKS PERSONAL GROWTH

The challenges and obstacles of civic engagement described by young people in this study were central to their personal development. While critical emotional challenges that pushed young people out of their emotional comfort zones were transformative turning points, participants also credited a complex system of adult support with their personal growth and development as global citizens. As they reflected on their civic experiences as a whole, they described their development as an unfolding journey of learning, skill improvement, personal awareness, and transformation.

Shifting from External to Internal Motivation

Pondering their civic journeys, the engaged youth in this study described a shift from external motivators to internal motivators. Those with the highest levels of commitment often talked about being drawn into community service in high school for external reasons, including resume-building, self-development, or meeting service requirements. Many young people spoke of these external motivators in their early years of service.

> To be honest, what really drew [me] to buy in and to call them is that they listed out everything that . . . we would benefit from. . . . We would get free food, . . . training, and be able to travel. . . . That was a big thing. —Scott

> At first . . . I had to do a certain number of community service hours a year. I was expected to and so it would fulfill my requirements. —Melinda

> I thought that service work was a very impersonal experience where you did some sort of almost arbitrary contribution to the community. . . . You go in, you get a T-shirt that says "volunteer" and then you move on and put it on your resume. —Danielle

Resolving Conflict between Self-Interest and Societal Concerns

As they were pushed to expand the boundaries of their thinking, young people often spoke of the conflict between self-interest and service beyond self, acknowledging that both played a role in their lives. Most students spoke of this internal conflict and an awareness of a shift from a focus on me to a focus on others.

> It definitely brought my world into perspective . . . no longer can I be selfish because there are people out there that are way worse off than me. —Ashley

What you want isn't best for everyone when you're just thinking about yourself. –Christina

When I first started [volunteering] . . . I wanted to help others and it was a great thing but it was also somewhat of a selfish move for me to benefit myself. . . . But now I do it more as me wanting to give to others and help others because I understand. –Scott

Defining Internal Motivators

Through their stories, students reported one or more of the intrinsic motivators in the graph below as reasons they sustain civic engagement. No differences were found between genders, religious preferences, socioeconomic groups, or political affiliations.

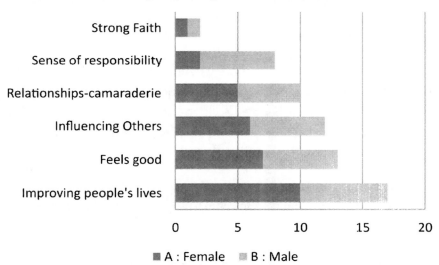

The following quotes are representative examples of each intrinsic motivator. Young people talked about improving people's lives as a primary motivator of engagement. In this category, half made a distinction between merely helping people and raising others to self-sufficiency.

That's what it was . . . a love for them and . . . a sincere desire that some-day they can go to school and . . . get an education that will help them be able to lead a better life than what their parents ended up leading. –Brook

Students also shared how good they felt when they volunteered, including the feelings of reward, accomplishment, and joy.

That's the best feeling in the world . . . when you accomplish something and you feel good inside about it. –Scott

Many students discussed how empowered they felt because they were able to influence others and make change.

I work towards encouraging them or influencing them to consider a dif-ferent way of thought, or actually realize that these issues are important in their life. –Rasheeda

Almost half made specific comments about the importance of rela-tionships and camaraderie to their motivation. The value of relation-ships with a variety of people, both adult and peers, was discussed in other findings related to meaning-making. It is likely most would agree with the following comment.

I would . . . emphasize some of the social aspects of what we do, because we don't do this in a bubble and could never do this without the people around us who are some of the best friends you'll make. –Amar

Some students talked about the sense of duty or responsibility they felt to be civically engaged. Several expressed guilt when they fell short of what they expected of themselves.

I feel like I'm upholding my civic duties in being an active, engaged cit-izen. –Jacqueline

While a handful of young people referred to their religious upbring-ing as being foundational to the development of moral values, only two expressed a strong faith in God as the motivational core of their service. In fact, most who listed church-related volunteer experiences on their resumes also self-identified as atheist/agnostic. Danielle, daughter of a preacher, provided a rich example of how faith motivated her actions in the world.

> A lot of it is faith-based, and stemming from that is a sense of responsibility to discreetly use the resources that we have and to be generous, and to take care of other people and help make sure that their needs are met. –Danielle

Gaining Personal Benefits

Each of the young people in this study reported significant intellectual, interpersonal, and intrapersonal benefits from their civic engagement experiences. Intellectually, they talked about how they learned to plan, organize, and solve problems. They did this both independently and collectively within groups. One of the biggest intellectual benefits was a gain in perspective. Youth learned to think critically about the world and understand the root causes of societal problems.

Young people also reflected on the growth of their relationship abilities—the interpersonal benefit of working in cooperative community service efforts. They learned to communicate and collaborate in environments outside of school—environments with real-world problems and consequences. They became good at motivating others toward social action, a key leadership skill for citizenship and advocacy.

Lastly, young people gained intrapersonal benefits— the feelings inside of themselves that motivated and energized all aspects of their lives. They grew in self-awareness and self-confidence. They felt compassion, respect, empathy, and optimism. Some reported a sense of patience, knowing it took time to make change in the world, but they felt content to take one step at a time.

The skills, abilities, and traits that were gained by participants as a result of their civic engagement experiences are depicted in the graph below.

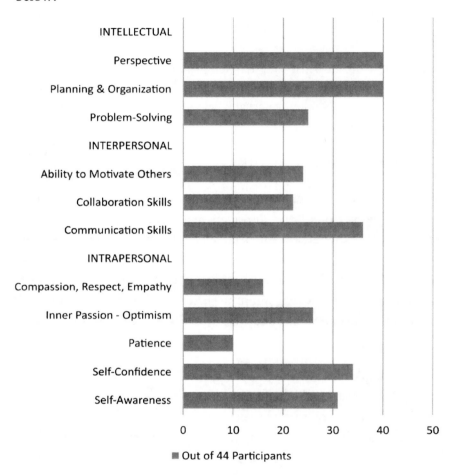

In almost all categories, the gains in development reported by those who participated in the survey only were closely related to the challenges and obstacles of civic engagement as described by those interviewed. For example, interviewees reported transformative experiences that significantly changed their perspectives on social issues as well as experiences of facing people with different worldviews. Therefore, it was not surprising to find that intellectual gains in perspective were reported by almost all participants. Similarly, interviewees reported challenges in the areas of planning, organization, and problem-solving—the same areas reported as developmental gains by those surveyed, but not interviewed.

In the area of interpersonal benefits, similar validation of interview data was found. For example, interviewees described communication and leadership challenges in their civic activities. These same themes of development showed up as top benefits gained by surveyed participants. While interviewees were most challenged by how to motivate others toward service, the ability to motivate others was cited by surveyed participants as an important gain in development.

Learning from Challenges and Obstacles

Further validating a link between the challenges and obstacles of civic engagement and developmental gains, most young people spoke more broadly about their valued learning and personal growth.

> So even though I've had very negative experiences . . . they are always experiences that have created the person I am today. –Ashley

> I think my experiences with [this organization] were very meaningful, despite my leaving at the end. I think had it not been for [them], I would not have developed my identity. –Ryan

> I was in this giant city not knowing anyone. But I think from that experience of being so scared and feeling so alone and not knowing how it's going to work out in Costa Rica, I would just say [to myself] . . . that "it's going to be fine." . . . It has helped me not to become so panicked when I'm in a place I don't know. And that really made me more confident and . . . independent. –Sarah

While young people described the challenges, transformative turning points, and adult support in previous sections, this section examined the slower, more long-term developmental progress described by young people. All participants reported significant developmental benefits as a result of civic activities, indicating that personal growth was a slow and evolving process. They described a gradual shift from being motivated by external reasons, like resume-building, to feeling motivated from within. This shift caused them to address conflicts between self-interest and service beyond self, acknowledging the importance of both in their lives.

Young people reported what motivated them to sustain civic engagement, including the desire to improve people's lives, influence others, and the simple fact that it felt good. In addition to describing intellectual, interpersonal, and emotional challenges of their work, students also reported developmental gains in each of these areas. The final section shifts from developmental benefits of engagement to explore how young people constructed meaning from their experiences—meaning that affected their civic actions in the world and inspired them to become innovators for social change.

MEANING-MAKING FUELS SOCIAL ACTION

While reflection was naturally part of the interview process, it was apparent that young people thought deeply about their civic engagement prior to this study. They reflected upon and discovered meaning from the challenges and obstacles they faced and from the relationships they experienced throughout their involvement in civic activities. Their learning gave purpose to their lives, motivated them to tackle challenging goals, and helped them believe in themselves and their abilities to make a difference in the world.

This section examines the similar threads of meaning young people found from very diverse civic experiences. First, it explores the common strategies participants used to engage others in civic causes. Second, it looks at the shared themes of their expanded worldviews.

Lastly, it describes how participants increased their sense of civic efficacy and gratitude for the education and opportunities given them.

Most young people interviewed for this study were highly reflective about their civic experiences and valued reflection as an important life process. Giovanni shared a particularly rich view of the importance of reflection and meaning-making in his life.

> Experience without reflection is only half the experience, and that's something I always remember because I understand that just doing something if I don't think about what it meant and think about it in the context of everything else that's going on in my life, it's not going to make as much sense to me. –Giovanni

Without exception, these young people expressed gratitude for the chance to participate in an interview for the study and saw it as an opportunity to further reflect on their lives. Most commented that the interview was extremely helpful to them, forcing them to think about the things that most mattered.

> It's just nice to get the chance to reflect and take time to remember. –Victor

> It's always a good thing to remind yourself of what your roots are, what you're doing, why you're doing it, the things that have inspired you. . . . reminding yourself of those things is really energizing. –Danielle

> You know, they're all things I think about and feel the impact of everyday. But to really go back there and sort of relive it as I'm talking to you, it's actually been pretty emotional, which I appreciate. I'm glad it's been that way. –Jennifer

Engaging Others in Social Change

When young people faced the challenge of motivating others to participate in civic causes, almost all of them used creative techniques that attempted to push others out of their comfort zones or inspire them to expand their boundaries. While no one ever directly related this approach to the meaning they discovered from their own out-of-comfort-zone or inspirational experiences, this theme appeared over and over again as young people lamented that others didn't have their experiences, but they wanted people to feel what they felt. Amar expressed this learning well. Ashley and Christina provided examples of their own efforts to push others to see issues from new perspectives.

> As I have progressed, it has been important to me to challenge people and get beyond the base feelings about their service. Sometimes this means putting people in an uncomfortable position or trying to get them to challenge each other. –Amar

> We'd always try to make the trash that we showed [in the video] the nastiest looking trash possible . . . tons of bottles everywhere . . . bottles piling up until the bottles officially disappear because people are recycling. –Ashley

> We have this thing called Shack-a-thon where we sleep in cardboard boxes in the middle of campus . . . to advocate that poverty is an issue everywhere. –Christina

Reshaping Worldviews

As noted earlier, almost all study participants reported a change in perspective or worldview as a result of their civic engagement activities. The meaning these young people discovered from their experiences was reflected in three important themes related to this perspective shift, that

1. Education brings about social change.
2. People have the same needs but not the same opportunities.
3. Face-to-face relationships and stories is what connects us to other human beings.

While these themes were more strongly articulated through in-depth conversations with interviewees, they were also validated through the narratives of those not interviewed. All interviewees talked about the meaning of education and appeared to have a systemic understanding of its impact.

> I believe a lack of adequate education to be a key factor in the majority of the problems we see in our society, so I think that if more children had better access to educations of a higher quality than what they currently receive, more people would be better able to solve their own problems or better equipped to help others. –Brook

> If we do not have adequate schooling, we will never be able to decrease poverty, crime, or other social problems that education can solve. –Jacqueline

Similar comments were found in the surveys of non-interviewed participants.

> I saw firsthand how much education benefits children of developing countries and how much hope it brings them. I truly believe in the philosophy to "help them help themselves." . . . If you give them an apple, they will grow an orchard to feed the whole village. This is why I am such a strong supporter of micro-financing, education, and skills training. –Susan

Regardless of their diverse family and socioeconomic backgrounds, all young people commented on their sense of privilege as U.S. citizens. They attributed civic experiences to shaping their beliefs that everyone deserves a decent life and that people have the same needs but not the same opportunities.

> The answer is that people who have privilege need to understand what it is like for people who do not have it. Homeless doesn't mean anything other than without an address. It reflects nothing of the moral character of the person. We cannot begin to understand the way that the world

works until we understand that people who have less than us are really no different. –Michael

Doing community service, you're able to see everyone as equal and you get to see that everyone struggles. . . . you become open minded. –Carlos

This theme also emerged in the surveys of non-interviewed participants.

So much of what we hear on the news makes us think that all immigrants are evil when, in fact, I did not find one evil being on my trip. The immigrant's work ethic and the immigrant's family orientation is what made me want to work for this group of people. –Luke

Most young people talked about the importance of face-to-face relationship building with people different from themselves and the powerful impact that stories have to foster understanding.

I found every single person I meet has a story. And just hearing those stories and learning from them, I think it makes my life a lot richer and a lot more interesting. –Melinda

The stories that they had were just fascinating and the lives that they led were so different from my own. And I felt like whenever I got to the farm, I became closer with them and heard a lot about their stories and learned a lot about the kind of life that I wanted to live. –Travis

This theme was validated by non-interviewed participants as they reflected on what they had gained from their civic experiences.

By working with others, I have learned that no matter how varied our lives are, by interacting and forging relationships with those different from ourselves, we are not only able to gain unique insight into our own lives, but the empathy necessary for a harmonious life. –Mariah

Finding a Sense of Civic Efficacy

As youth reflected on themselves through the lens of their civic experiences, all described a sense of civic efficacy, a belief that they can make a difference in the world. They often recalled their early years of community service, when it was difficult to understand that small actions could make big differences in people's lives. They described changes in those feelings over time as they became more aware. Surprisingly, for young people who made such large contributions through service, they seemed highly motivated by small successes. This feeling was expressed by all of the students interviewed.

And I didn't realize the tiniest things that I could be doing to help other people. –Ashley

You can't completely eradicate the problem. . . . But every dent helps, every minute that you're out there helping matters. –Christina

It makes you kind of live with a sense of urgency to know that even your attitude can have that kind of effect on someone and make them more effective participants in the community. –Danielle

I'm not going to have that direct connection to be able to treat the person who can't afford to go to the hospital, but . . . I can study health policy and try to find ways it can be implemented so that person . . . can have things easier. –Ethan

I've learned more about how I can personally make a difference. . . . The fight against poverty is something that's incomprehensible. It's so much bigger than me. . . . Before I started working with [the One Campaign] it [wasn't] something that motivated [me]. . . . it just seemed too big. But [this work] has really made me realize that each person does make a giant difference. . . . Whether it's signing a petition or visiting a member of Congress, calling your Senator, or just things like that. –Sarah

Feeling Grateful

The other important change in self that was reflected in most students interviewed was the development of a deep sense of gratitude for their education and opportunities.

> I [feel] incredibly fortunate for whatever reason people have trusted me and given me these experiences, given me the gift of these opportunities, [without which] I would not be the person that I am today. –Jared

> I would say I feel very blessed as an individual, and not everybody is . . . not everybody is given the same opportunities. –Jacqueline

> I think that the thing I've taken away from it the most is something I think about probably at least three times a day, is how incredibly lucky I am to have the opportunity for the education that I'm getting. –Melinda

This sense of gratitude was also expressed in surveys of non-interviewed participants.

> Coming from a small, homogeneous and affluent community, having the opportunity to interact with others from different backgrounds and social histories has allowed me to see just how fortunate I am, and to never take what my life has offered me for granted. –Mariah

> I have been able to attend my first-choice college as the first in my family to attend a high-level learning institution. I have met similarly-minded, passionate, engaged individuals that have shaped my passions and broadened my worldview—individuals that otherwise are hard to come by. –Lauren

Young people found meaning from their civic experiences that gave purpose to their lives and motivated them to tackle challenging societal issues. They welcomed opportunities for self-reflection, including the chance to be interviewed for this study. Surprisingly, they described similar threads of meaning from quite diverse experiences. In efforts to engage others in civic causes, they used creative strategies that pushed people out of their comfort zones and inspired them to expand the boundaries of their thinking.

Civic learning resulted in three shared perspectives: that education was a driving force in positive social change; that people have the same needs, but not the same opportunities; and that face-to-face relationships with others are critical. Not only did young people believe they could make a difference in the world, but they found meaning in small everyday occasions to serve causes greater than themselves. Recognizing not every young person had the same chances in life; participants expressed gratitude for their education and unique opportunities for learning.

CHAPTER SUMMARY

This study explored the life experiences and circumstances that helped adolescents sustain civic engagement in the face of challenges and obstacles. Findings suggested a relationship between experiencing these challenges and the development of civically engaged youth. For the young adults in this study, the journey to becoming innovative, engaged citizens was a slow, evolving process filled with learning, skill development, self-discovery, and transformation. Below is a short summary of the five themes discussed in this chapter:

1. Civic Engagement is Challenging

Young people described three types of challenges encountered through civic or political activities. *Intellectual challenges* were highly related to developmental gains in critical thinking, planning, organizing, and problem solving. *Interpersonal challenges* provided opportunities to work collaboratively, improve communication skills, and motivate others. Young people also learned from the *emotional chal-*

lenges of civic engagement, those that pushed them out of their emotional comfort zones and caused them to confront moral issues.

2. Emotional Connection Matters Most

It was the emotional challenges that helped young people develop internal strengths such as compassion, empathy, inner passion, optimism, patience, self-confidence and self-awareness. These kinds of challenges, often associated with transformative experiences, were related to the development of a sense of purpose and motivated young people to adopt specific civic causes. Learning gained as a result of civic challenges and obstacles seemed to fuel young people's initiative for social action.

3. Adult Support is Essential

Adult scaffolding played a significant role in the lives of all young people in this study. Findings suggested that adult mentors, civic role models, parents, and program leaders played key and differing roles. Almost all young people had non-parent adult mentors with whom they had long-term relationships. These mentors, most often educators, helped instill a belief in self without which many said they would not be the people they were today. The role of civic role models was inspirational, providing sources of motivation and examples to follow. Findings suggested that parents provided scaffolding for the moral development of their children. Many kinds of programs were rich environments for transformative learning. Program leaders supplied opportunities to expand critical thinking, problem-solving, and interpersonal skills. Like adult mentors and parents, they also reinforced moral values and encouraged and supported students as they faced challenges and obstacles.

4. Giving Back Sparks Personal Growth

All participants reported big developmental gains as a result of civic activities, indicating a perception that they received far more than what they gave. Students described a gradual shift from being motivated by external reasons, like resume-building, to feeling motivated from within. This shift caused them to address conflicts between self-interest and service beyond self, acknowledging the importance of both in their lives.

5. Meaning-Making Fuels Social Action

Self-reflection and meaning making played an important role in developing young people's civic identity. Young people thought deeply about their personal beliefs through the lens of their civic experiences. They struggled with moral dilemmas and intentionally reflected on the meaning of service beyond self. The reflection and meaning-making process caused young people to expand their worldviews, increase their belief that they could make a difference in the world, and engage others in civic causes. It fostered a deep gratitude for their education and opportunities, brought purpose to their lives, and motivated them to tackle challenging goals in the future.

5

Learning that Transforms Lives

For those of us who want to see democracy survive and thrive—and we are legion—the heart is where everything begins: that grounded place in each of us where we can overcome fear, rediscover that we are members of one another, and embrace the conflicts that threaten democracy as openings to new life for us and for our nation.

— Parker J. Palmer, *Healing the Heart of Democracy:*
The Courage to Create a Politics Worthy of the Human Spirit

When service touches young people's hearts, something powerful occurs. They begin to see themselves as part of a world much larger than themselves.

In their most memorable community service experiences, the young adults in my study recalled defining, heartfelt moments—times when they felt empathy for others at whole new levels. These feelings of deep human connection initiated a process that quite literally trans-formed young people's lives. They were catalysts that brought out the best in them, defining them as young Americans with a passion to make a difference.

The most striking fact about life's defining moments—which can never be fully grasped or understood—is just how short they are. They are brief flashes in a lifetime of moments. For the young people who talked openly about their most meaningful volunteer experiences, defining moments were often mere seconds of deep empathetic connection with other human beings. Yet those seconds created lasting impacts on how they would eventually transform empathy into action in the world.

All of us can recall defining moments in our lives. We often think of them as big, life-changing events like when we fall in love, have a child, change careers, or lose someone we love. Sometimes they happen unexpectedly and other times we prepare for them. But always, we seem to reflect back on how these critical life events defined our identities and life purpose. Just as these bigger, life-altering moments occur for all of us, there are also more nuanced moments that define our identities as caring individuals and citizens. Those moments, and the stories that lead up to them, always involve our innate ability to interact with others emotions—to experience empathy.

The young people I interviewed demonstrated beautifully how their relationships and experiences during childhood and adolescence triggered these more nuanced moments during service projects in high school—moments that increased their abilities to care for groups of individuals. In turn, their heightened levels of empathy motivated them to work toward causes bigger than themselves.

While we may want to believe these moments are rare and unpredictable, we now know that the brain is wired for them to occur. With the right guidance and practice during childhood, these moments can trigger enormous growth and learning during the teen years. The difference between the adolescents in this book and many of their peers is that the students I studied were emotionally ready to embrace their defining moments and were also prepared with the skills to glean meaning from them.

In Chapter 4, the results of my study were presented in thematic categories. Young people shared common insights despite a wide range of civic learning experiences, backgrounds, and ethnicity. This chapter explores a handful of their stories in greater depth, with a special emphasis on transformative learning, a concept that evolves throughout the chapter. While the summaries in Chapter 4 were derived from strict coding of narrative data, this chapter recognizes the more relational role between the researcher and participants.

RELATIONAL LEARNING

Throughout a child's growing-up years, their relationships with family, teachers, friends, and mentors merge with their life experiences in ways that prepare them for critical moments of learning during adolescence. Ashley's story is particularly poignant because it so clearly demonstrates this phenomenon. Early in my interview with Ashley, a high school senior, she mentioned that her Mom was a single parent. Later, after she discussed her volunteer experiences, I returned to ask more about her family.

From Ashley's vivacious manner and the confidence she exuded when speaking of her desire to major in digital media at the University of Central Florida, I expected to hear a fairly typical and even amiable middle-class divorce story. But the particulars of Ashley's story—and the perspective she was able to bring to it—took me by surprise.

As if to shield me from anticipated awkwardness, Ashley instantly let me know it was okay to ask questions about her family, saying, "I'm extremely comfortable discussing that my dad is addicted to crack cocaine and is in prison. My dad is part of my life, but he was doing drugs before I was even born. And all of our family money was put towards his addiction. When I was five, my parents got divorced."

Ashley continued to describe her childhood, admitting her dad "wasn't a huge part of my life because he was in and out of jail throughout those years and not really there for me. When he was there, it was definitely a very difficult time. But I still have a relationship with my dad." Pausing as if she had just remembered something important, her voice became more cheerful, saying, "Today is actually his birthday." And then with a deep breath, she more softly acknowledged that "the timing of our interview is ironic," because her father's birthday coincided with this unexpected opportunity to reflect about the challenges she overcame as a result of his life choices.

I took a deep breath too, because at that moment I knew I had connected with a remarkable 18-year-old who would teach me important lessons about caring and compassion. As a mother myself, I felt a flash of empathy with Ashley's mom. When I asked about her, Ashley's response was not surprising. "Oh my goodness," she said, "She is my hero!" Her mom was a model of strength and resiliency throughout very difficult years. After losing a family cleaning business because of her husband's drug habit, Ashley's mom worked a number of jobs while raising three children. Ashley admitted that divorcing her dad "was something my mom did to better the lives of me and my brothers. Seeing her to be such a strong, independent individual impacted me immensely."

Rather than blaming others, Ashley's mother taught her children that difficult situations required hard work and perseverance. One evening a week, Ashley's mother took her kids with her to help clean apartments, houses, and places of business. "We did it together as a family," Ashley said, "and my mom would always buy us kids Slurpees as compensation."

Caring Home Environments

By most standards, Ashley's childhood was challenging. She acknowledged, "My family did not have many luxuries. I knew my life was difficult." She and her family also helped clean their church building and Ashley said, "They helped us out a little bit financially." Reminiscing about those days with more enthusiasm than I expected, she exclaimed, "We made cleaning fun! One of the buildings had two stories, so we would end up with piles of trash on the second floor above the dumpster. Then we would toss the trash bags," making a game out of throwing them at a target!

While Ashley's life was difficult, her mother was still able to provide the type of nurturing home environment that other young people described as being essential to developing positive values. Ashley spoke of how her mom "showed us how to help others." Jokingly, she said, "My Mom loves feeding people, so it came by my family naturally to volunteer at food banks." When she was young, she remembers, "just seeing other people volunteering and how much excitement it brought into their lives" was inspiring. This type of environment invited Ashley to reflect on difficult situations, seek guidance from supportive adults, and integrate tough experiences into her life in healthy ways. As a result, Ashley said, "I never look back at negative experiences with regrets. They are experiences that created the person I am today."

So often, when we hear stories like Ashley's we expect less optimal outcomes. Yet, with great sincerity, Ashley believed she had "the most open family you could ever imagine." She illustrated this as she spoke fondly of her mother, brothers, and even her father, knowing that she "could discuss anything with them."

Connecting with Mentors

As Ashley described aspects of her growing up years, it was clear how the atmosphere of easy conversation at home helped her become open and responsive to other adults who could take her under wing. For example, a close friend introduced Ashley to Mrs. Mary Erickson, a professional photographer. Mary, with two daughters of her own, took an interest in Ashley and encouraged her "to get involved in several volunteer organizations." She also supported Ashley's interest in digital media by inviting her to assist in some of her photography sessions. "I would hold the reflector for her," Ashley said, and "help her in other ways too."

As Ashley's relationship with Mrs. Erickson grew, "Eventually, she hired me to work at different nonprofit events at her home. I would help greet, give people name tags, and make sure the food was ready." These kinds of experiences gave Ashley self confidence in public arenas outside of school and family. As Ashley reflected on the mentoring and opportunities she received, she proclaimed, "I adore Mrs. Erickson! She was clearly a positive impact in my life!" Indeed, Mrs. Erickson was the kind of non-parent mentor that all of the young people I interviewed described as vital to the caring individuals they became.

Like most teens, Ashley felt a lot of stress in high school to get good grades. She recalled one day after school when she was the lead producer of a video production, and at the same time, juggling to study for a history exam on the Civil War, a subject she considered her worst. "My history questions made no sense to me," she said, and she felt paralyzed with so many tasks to accomplish. Mr. Andres, her film teacher, mentored Ashley's interest in learning to produce television programs. But on this particular day, Mr. Andres "could tell something was definitely wrong with me." As soon as he said, "You seem to have a lot on your plate," Ashley recalled that his words "opened up the lines of communication," and her exasperation poured out like "word vomit."

Admittedly, the phrase "word vomit" hit me hard. As I reviewed the transcripts of all my interviews over and over again, I was struck by the pressure that most kids feel in today's school environments. Like Ashley, they looked to their teachers for support and guidance.

"It was so nice," Ashley said, "to have someone who could see I was under a lot of stress and to care enough to ask me about it and to coach me through it." What followed was the mark of an exceptional mentor. Mr. Andres helped Ashley prioritize her tasks, encouraging her to see the steps involved, particularly when there are many competing projects. "He helped me look at everything from a bigger perspective, which is difficult for me whenever I get overwhelmed," she said. "And then, he started talking to me about history. But best of all, he went through his box of old videos created by students, pulled out one on the Civil War, and had me sit down and watch it. This was the best way to relate to me—to see it through television!"

No matter what the subject, teachers who know their students also understand how they learn and how to coach them through emotional meltdowns. Ashley admitted, "It wasn't necessarily like I knew all of the answers for my history exam. But I didn't seem so overwhelmed by it. I knew everything was going to be okay." As Ashley reflected on what she had learned from Mr. Andres' mentoring, she spoke very confidently about problem-solving, "It's not about just focusing on every little tiny aspect, which is obviously important, but it's about stepping back and looking at the whole problem."

Photographer Mrs. Erickson and teacher Mr. Andres may not have even realized how their small actions paid big dividends for Ashley's ability to develop empathy and to eventually turn empathy into action. Both adults took an interest in Ashley outside of classrooms or after-school activities, letting her know they valued her as a person. They are examples of the kinds of attachment relationships during adolescence that stimulate the brain's neuroplasticity. These relationships increase a child's ability to learn and also help them believe in themselves.

Despite a multitude of childhood obstacles, Ashley had developed strong, empathy-based relationships with adults who prepared her well for what she might encounter when she began to push her comfort zone as an adolescent. They helped her gain confidence, reflect on what mattered most in life, and persevere despite challenges. These skills had been nurtured by her family, teachers, mentors, and community leaders who instilled positive values, provided valuable learning opportunities, and gave her appropriate guidance along the way.

Like the other young people who shared their stories with me, supportive adults showed up in Ashley's life, modeled effective ways to overcome challenges, helped her gain perspective, and spent time mentoring her when she needed guidance. Consequently, by the time she reached adolescence, she was well-prepared to push her own emotional comfort zone—ready to define herself as a caring, empathetic, and civically-engaged person.

GATEWAYS TO DEEP UNDERSTANDING

During the teen years, the frontal area of the brain manages the process of developing empathy and shaping moral behavior. It is also capable of increased levels of reflective thinking and decision making, helping teenagers more deeply understand themselves and take action on their beliefs. As I interviewed students about their most meaningful volunteer experiences during high school, each one of them could easily describe a defining moment—a heartfelt connection with someone different from themselves—that created a gateway to these deeper levels of empathy. This key encounter motivated them to become engaged in helping others and contributing to society.

Like millions of teenagers, Ashley volunteered her time with various organizations during her growing up years. Because her family had a positive experience with hospice as her grandmother was dying of cancer, she decided to volunteer with a hospice program. Mostly, she "would go into the office and help with paperwork and different projects like making copies." Other times, she "would go into the actual Hospice House where there were patients" and she would "be there to greet and answer the phone." But she "never really felt connected at the Hospice House." Like many other teens her age, volunteering seemed more like just another activity, an experience to add to a college resume.

Linking Youth Interests with Life-Changing Experiences

Ashley thought of quitting her job with hospice, but instead courageously asked if there was any other type of work she could do. This was an opening for an adult to get to know Ashley's skills and involve her in more stimulating ways. At the time, Ashley was studying videography and thought she might be interested in a career in television. When the hospice coordinator learned of these skills, she asked if Ashley would like to help videotape dying patients as they talked about their lives. She would be expected to "create a video of their life along with music and still pictures." Her video would then be given to the family as a keepsake.

Sadly, many adult volunteers who supervise high school students would not have taken the time to link Ashley's interest in video with the potential for such deep learning. Most teens I spoke with complained that adults don't take their skills or potential contributions seriously. They get pigeon-holed in meaningless jobs that fail to connect them with the organization's greater mission. As many described in their interviews, this connection is exactly what they most need in order to learn the true meaning of service. Once they feel connected at deeper emotional levels, even minor tasks don't seem trivial anymore.

For Ashley, this project sounded like "an incredible experience." Anticipating the assignment pushed her out of her emotional comfort zone, something teen brains crave. "I was afraid I wouldn't be able to portray the person properly," she said. "I was very hesitant about going into their houses to meet with them and their families." Along with her "nerves and anxiousness" about the project itself, Ashley would also come face-to-face with dying patients. Would this be too much for a 16-year-old to handle?

Guidance from Supportive Adults

If Ashley had been placed into this situation alone, her story might have ended differently. But accompanying her was a caring adult who had previously videotaped patients for the project. As a result, the logistics of her first taping went quite smoothly. A hospice worker did the interviewing while Ashley operated the video equipment. A good final product was assured for the family.

The emotional aspects of Ashley's tasks were not as simple or straightforward. Not surprisingly for her age, Ashley tried to shield herself from what was really happening during the filming—the deeper aspects of dying and of leaving a living memory for loved ones. "I wasn't focused on the moment. I was just worried about the product—and about my camera batteries dying."

In the midst of her worry and anxiousness, Ashley's moment of deep learning was about to occur. At the end of the video session, she approached the hospice patient "to say goodbye" and was greeted with an unexpected hug. The patient, with tears rolling down his face, said, "Thank you so much for being here and caring about me."

In that instant, Ashley felt changed by her experience. "All of a sudden, I was like, wow!" said Ashley. "I was way too selfish. I was focused on myself and my equipment rather than the situation I was in. That's when the moment sunk in. I felt how thankful this person was that I was there and how much it meant to him. I learned it's the small things that matter. That's when everything started to kick in that this was such an important situation I was involved in."

This powerful, empathetic encounter with a dying patient became Ashley's defining moment—a moment she often reflected upon during the next few years. It was a moment of deep caring, where she connected with someone who was different from herself. It is these deep emotional connections that stimulate neuroplasticity and learning. And it is this empathetic encounter that pushed Ashley's emotional boundaries and opened up a reflective process in the prefrontal cortex of her teen brain. Through a brief moment with a dying man, Ashley found herself on the threshold of meaning—about to define her own values and beliefs.

Before leaving for college, Ashley was not only videotaping dying patients, she was also interviewing them. "I was there at the foot of the bed, still anxious, but talking with family members." After she set up her equipment, she remembers asking questions like "Where did they grow up? What did they do in high school? It was incredible how many things they were able to remember, how many stories they were telling!" No longer was Ashley's focus on her equipment—it was on a dying individual who had led a memorable and cherished life. Her experience fueled her ability to care at deeper levels and to use her creative talents to benefit others.

TRANSFORMING EMPATHY
INTO CIVIC LEARNING

What Ashley gained from her work with dying patients is what psychologists call transformative learning—learning that is linked with deep meaning and action. This kind of learning is known to develop internal purpose (Kovan & Dirkx, 2003) and involves a shift in how individuals see themselves, their relationships, and the world around them (Morrell & O'Connor, 2002). For Ashley, the emotional connection with one dying man caused her to see all dying people differently, connect their stories with why she volunteered, and find purpose in her work as a videographer. With a greater sense of meaning, even the small tasks at the hospice center took on new importance.

Transformative learning has been studied for more than two decades by researchers interested in how adults change and develop through the lifespan (Mezirow, 1991). The process usually begins with a challenge that perches us at the edge of our comfort zones, like Ashley's experience with videotaping a dying patient. While we feel some risk and vulnerability, it is also a catalyst for learning and personal growth. As we move forward, we discover meaning that causes us to change perspectives. Research studies link transformative learning to positive action and help us understand how people grow from experiences that test their abilities to overcome life's obstacles (Taylor, 2007).

The study on which this book is based broke new ground, finding that teenagers, regardless of their backgrounds, experience transformation and growth through processes similar to those of their adult counterparts. Adolescents recounted these transformative experiences over and over again, describing how they learned to care for others and discover personal meaning that fueled their civic engagement. Most recalled these turning points between the ages of 15 and 19, during emotional challenges they faced while serving their communities. These challenges involved their ability to feel other people's feelings.

While the details of their stories are understandably different, these high school students shared a common learning process—a process that took them to deeper levels of empathy and understanding. Each defining moment also helped them explore their own values in new ways. As they drew courage and strength from supportive adults, these experiences helped them choose their own paths toward becoming caring young people who walked their talk in the world. The students I interviewed connected five phases of personal growth with their most meaningful volunteer opportunities.

FIVE PHASES OF TRANSFORMATIVE LEARNING

When young people described their defining moments and how those moments affected their lives, they did so with a deep sense of meaning and gratitude. The first phase of transformative learning always began when youth connected at human boundaries, primarily through face-to-face relationships with people who were different from them. Quite literally, they stepped into a world unlike the one they knew. Their connection with people they met in this different world drew on their abilities to sense feelings in response to others' emotions, what neuroscientists call affective empathy.

For example, some students connected with a homeless person for the first time. On the inside, this felt risky and challenging, and pushed them out of their emotional comfort zones. In this different world, they began to confront their values, the second phase of their learning process. They reached back into their childhoods to what they had learned about good vs. evil, right vs. wrong, and compassion vs. hatred. This thought process occurred because they were suddenly faced with a more grown-up moral dilemma—homelessness. They felt confused because what they had been taught didn't always jive with what they were feeling at the moment. It took time to sort through these values and most often caused them to ask questions about their own privilege.

The third phase in this learning process forced young people to reflect on meaning, where they asked, "Who am I in relationship to my values?" They decided what was "right" for them to believe as an individual and how they might live their values in the world. This was often an agonizing and painful time, and usually the phase where adult mentors played an important role. However, teens agreed that support that was merely a display of comfort was not enough. Instead, they needed adults to be okay with their struggle, to help them sustain the courage needed to live at the edge of their comfort zones until they found resolution. This was the type of support that also helped them believe in themselves.

As young people gleaned meaning from their experience, they began to change and integrate their perspectives, the fourth phase in the process. For example, they connected homelessness to other social issues, like education, mental illness, or poverty. These were new insights involving cognitive empathy, the brain's ability to more fully identify and understand people who are different from us. Before this transformative process, they may have believed homeless people were dangerous, uneducated addicts. Now they saw them as human beings just like them, only without an address.

With a new sense of empathy and belief in their abilities, young people felt internally motivated to live and lead from a place of caring and compassion for themselves and others. This last phase of the process was most exhilarating as young people were compelled through their own feelings of empathy to engage in meaningful civic goals. These goals not only included a specific commitment to social or environmental issues, but also deeply informed their college and career choices.

When we support young people through these five phases of transformative learning, we prepare them to tackle and learn from challenges they will face as adults. We give them something grades cannot—the ability to reach inside themselves, access empathy, and live their values in the world. Community service provides unique opportunities in which to experience transformative learning because it has the potential to push kids out of their comfort zones to confront the values that lie at the heart of who they are as individuals. As a result, they discover inner strengths that increase their learning and resiliency.

As parents, educators, and counselors, we would much prefer young people develop empathy and purpose as the result of positive life experiences. But we have a dilemma. Where do young people learn the skills they need to overcome big, unexpected challenges in life if we don't provide opportunities for them to do so in safe environments where they can learn from their mistakes?

Learning that has the potential to transform young lives always begins at an emotional edge—a place where they feel uncomfortable. The teenagers in this book were prepared to learn from the challenges they found at this edge. Based on research in child and adolescent development, most children should be able to learn from these emotional challenges by the age of 15. Sadly though, we are not preparing children to reach these transformative turning points—opportunities that not only increase empathy, but also build other social, emotional, and cognitive skills.

More than any other activity, work in one's own community has been shown to develop skills that lead to transformative learning. But it's not as simple as giving young people a task, explaining how it's done, and recording their hours of service. To help understand how service facilitates the development of empathy and purpose, the following stories illustrate several young people's journeys through these transformative phases.

CONNECTING WITH PEOPLE
FROM DIFFERENT BACKGROUNDS

Travis, a young man from the Boston suburbs, talked about the importance of connecting as he described his experiences in the summer of his junior year of high school. He said, "I had a lot of free time on my hands, so I asked myself, 'Why am I not doing anything with my time when I know there's an activity I could be doing?'" On further reflection, Travis admitted, "In many ways, I guilt-tripped myself into volunteering." Wanting to be outdoors, he decided to volunteer at an organic farm in an agricultural community a short distance from his home. While being outdoors was pleasant and familiar, he knew the people who worked in this particular community were not as affluent as those from his own neighborhood. At first, Travis felt ill at ease in these new surroundings.

"The people I worked with at the farm," Travis said, "were really inspiring to me. The whole way they lived their lives was really different. The kinds of backgrounds they came from were very different from my own. Whenever I got to the farm, I became closer with them, listened to their stories, and learned a lot about the kind of life I wanted to live."

Like Travis, other young people talked about the power of people's stories over and over again, and how stories helped them connect to what was important in their own lives. This finding would not be surprising to scholars who have linked storytelling to meaning-making for many years (Polkinghorne, 1988). It is through people's stories that we develop our own views of the world. When we interact with people whose stories are different than our own, it forces us to reexamine our values and perceptions. For adolescents, it fosters the development of their identities.

I asked Travis to imagine a day at the farm, and if he could, paint a picture in words to describe one of the interactions that stood out for him where he learned a different way of thinking or being. He responded, "Yeah, absolutely! Since it is an organic farm, almost all the work is done by hand. One of the most needed activities is weeding—pretty much straight-up work with your hands in the dirt. I remember a conversation with Rosa, the garden coordinator. She said, 'Oh, I love weeding. I could just do it all day.' I knew Rosa was smart and I knew what she had to say was really valuable, but I never thought about how weeding could be fun! I don't think she was trying to say this in a Tom Sawyer style to get me to treat my work differently. But she really did teach me something about weeding—appreciating it, enjoying working with my hands, and feeling it."

Connecting with people who see the world differently, even in small ways, affects young people's lives. Not only do they absorb new ways of thinking and feeling, but they share pride from their learning with families, friends, and others around them. Travis said, "Quite literally, I got value from getting dirty! I left the farm dirty every day. I'd usually go back to a local pool where I worked and I'd take a shower. Everyone would ask me about what I had done and why I was so dirty, and I'd say, 'Oh you know, I work at this farm,' and I'd feel kind of proud of myself. It was really foreign to everybody. And, at the time, it became part of my identity."

Pushing Young People's Emotional Comfort Zones

Like Travis, the stories shared by other young people in this book show us that the potential for learning and personal growth is heightened when teenagers connect with others at the edges of their comfort zones. When we think of these edges as perceived intellectual, social, or emotional boundaries, we begin to deepen our understanding of the types of environments that help young people learn from the inside out and grow to become engaged members of their families, work places, and communities.

Scientists have studied the relationship between learning and connecting at boundaries for decades. In fact, it was first recognized in the 1950's that the nooks, crannies, and peripheries between people, organizations, and their environments were fertile areas of growth (Bertalanffy, 1956). The potential for learning in these areas is the result of unexplained collaborative processes inherent in groups of individuals working together. These processes, since linked to problem-solving, innovation, and social change (Fagerberg, 2004), cannot be measured by grades and test scores.

I was surprised by how well the young people in my study articulated the importance of connecting at boundaries and how those connections became the transformative beginnings to more deeply learning about themselves. Like Travis' new understanding of weeding, another young man learned first-hand that building houses in New Orleans was more than "just gutting a home." As he reflected on the emotional challenges of his work, he stated with absolute assertion, "It's that connection to the people."

The young people I interviewed experienced their deepest moments of learning when they felt out of their comfort zones, connecting to others who were significantly different from them. Most described coming face-to-face with less privileged people as being extremely challenging, uncomfortable, and perspective-changing. Some, like Travis, talked about connecting with the environment through people who lived very different lifestyles than themselves. Many, like Ashley, described encounters with people who were dying, disabled, or suffering. And some crossed boundaries to experience deep learning at youth gatherings that were highly structured with transformative learning in mind.

One student summarized it well, "You can't ignore a situation when it's put out right in front of you. When you see something on TV, you can just change the channel. Or if you read about something, you can just close the book. But when it's right in front of you, it's really hard to ignore." Young people agreed it was the process of connecting to others on a deep, personal level that challenged them toward the next phase in their transformative journeys.

CONFRONTING PERSONAL VALUES

Jared, a student from the Pacific Northwest, beautifully illustrated the second phase of transformative learning—how teens confront their values when they connect with people different from themselves. Jared had participated in a number of activities in his top-ranked public high school that "were taking a lot of time," but where "we never talked about our personal experiences." Then he signed up for a community-sponsored month-long summer travel program in Russia that included working with two groups of Russian orphans, each for four days. "It gave me a window into lives that were incredibly different from my own. And it was an experience that changed my life and the way I saw the world."

Like all the young people who shared their stories, the process of confronting values was complex for Jared. It involved multidimensional layers of non-linear thinking—thinking that progressed organically rather than in a step-by-step, cause-and-effect manner. He thought deeply about the kids in the orphanage, the American counselors, and the underlying values of the program itself. The process was agonizing.

I asked Jared questions about the aspects of the orphanage experience that were most challenging for him. "Well," he said, "the hardest part was becoming really attached to another human being. When the kids left at the end of camp, I knew I would never see them again. But I also had a general sense of how hard their lives would be in ways they didn't create for themselves. And that was really hard to swallow."

Jared described more about his four days with the orphans. "There was lots of interaction and playing together. But my campers were my responsibility. I would watch out for them, help make sure they were having a good time, and give them affection. Four days doesn't sound like a long time, but it was an intense experience."

I asked Jared more about his feelings after leaving the orphanage and how the program benefited the children. "I thought a lot about that and struggled with that very issue. It was an intense four days, but four days is still only four days! It was on my mind at the time and long afterwards. What does this do for them in the long run?"

As Jared struggled with the answer to his own question, his hope was that the children "would look back in a dark moment and remember a happy time." In the short term, "I think what we were doing for them was just letting them be children for four days. I think that was the gift we gave them, because their regular lives were really difficult."

Jared then told me a story about one of the boys in the orphanage who helped him challenge his values about good vs. bad people. "One of my campers was a nine-year-old boy. He was really tough, and the only emotions he showed were anger or uninhibited pleasure. He picked on other kids and was sometimes violent. Some of the kids were really affectionate, but he certainly was not. But his personal history was that he had been abused by his father who was an alcoholic, and he had this terribly troubled home life before he was put in the orphanage. As I was saying goodbye to him, I had these strong feelings that he was going to become a person that I would look at in 20 years and think, 'he's a bad man.'"

Being with this young boy forced Jared to rethink his ideas of what makes people good or evil. Was this orphan responsible for being violent? Were adults responsible? Was society to blame? "In what standard, or what system of evaluation, was he really responsible?" asked Jared with strong emotion. "The behavior he had been taught was okay to him." Jared returned from Russia thinking that "humans are responsible for each other and this web of responsibility is complex and deep."

Drawing on Internal Strengths to Define Beliefs

Like other students who had been immersed in similar programs, Jared struggled with how to communicate about his experience when he returned home. Because he had traveled with high school classmates, those students became very comfortable talking about their experiences together. "So in a lot of ways," Jared admitted, "being really close with everyone was incredible. But in other ways, it was really difficult because it put strain on other relationships."

Confused, and with a myriad of feelings, Jared was forced to figure out what he valued in friendships, how he viewed people with less privilege, the definition of good and evil, and much more. This is exactly the type of work that adolescent development theorists like Erik Erikson spoke about as being critical for teens as they transition to adulthood. Erikson claimed this period of life drew on prior internal strengths and how young people used those strengths to face challenges and obstacles in the real world. This process, he claimed, helped young people define the differences between good and evil, and develop a sense of morality that remained with them for a life-time (Erikson, 1958).

Jared's parents could afford to send him on an international adventure, but teenagers don't have to travel to Siberia to connect with people different from themselves to question the values on which they build their identities. However, exchange programs with other countries have become a popular way to expose adolescents to unfamiliar and extremely challenging environments that have potential for transformative learning. Despite a wide range of family income levels, many of the students in this book spoke, like Jared, of programs in developing countries as pivotal experiences that helped them confront their values.

When adolescents connect through empathy with people who push them out of their comfort zones, they are naturally forced to examine their own values. Empathy becomes a doorway to compassion and kindness, but only through an internal struggle to find their own answers. During this time, adolescents reach back into their childhoods for guidance to the relationships and experiences that fostered positive values like honesty, integrity, and self-responsibility. The young people I interviewed had families, teachers, and after-school program leaders who fostered these values. That made them well-prepared to learn from the out-of-comfort-zone experiences they encountered in their service projects as teenagers.

Defining values and personal beliefs are at the core of adolescent development theory. Everything before this time prepares children for their social roles and how they fit into society. For example, we teach elementary and middle school children how to be responsible citizens—why they should be kind to others, recycle trash, and do their homework. But teenagers must move beyond a feeling of mere responsibility to merge what they have learned about social roles with who they want to become. Their two identities—social and psychological—must join together during adolescence, a uniting of self and society (Erikson, 1950). For Jared and others, community service provided the opportunity for them to confront their values in ways that helped them merge these two identities.

REFLECTING ON MEANING

Like most teens, Ryan, now a sophomore at Tufts University, struggled to express himself in high school in ways that felt comfortable to him. Soft-spoken yet assertive, he talked about not wanting to "be confrontational" with people because he didn't want them "to be turned off by what I said." Today, Ryan is a talented rapper who was able to speak articulately about how he developed self-reflection skills as an adolescent.

Curious about his Chinese roots, Ryan decided to join an Asian youth organization. Not its real name, I'll refer to this organization as AYO for short. Describing the group's mission, Ryan said, "AYO taught its members about Asian-American history and how to empower Asian teens to better understand their culture." He attributes his participation in this group to "developing my Asian-American identity."

Before Ryan connected with AYO, he struggled with how he fit into society. From a middle-class Asian-American family, he contemplated his place in the world. "I realized I wasn't White. I'm not this—and I'm not that. I didn't think I wanted to be part of the dominant group, but at the same time, I just didn't know." Over the next year and a half, being a member of AYO helped Ryan internalize what it meant for him to be Asian and American.

Connecting with AYO pushed Ryan to ask important questions about himself. But it also led to a difficult moral dilemma. "The coordinator always encouraged us to protest and go to rallies," he revealed. It was emphasized that "one of our main priorities in coming to this program was to speak up and demand what was right." As time went on, Ryan grew uncomfortable, and admittedly a bit angry, with the idea that an organization could always be "right." This was when Ryan connected with people different from him and was forced to confront his values.

The deeper he looked inside himself, Ryan said, "I started thinking about what they were doing. They were not really teaching us how to think, but what to think. Sometimes I joke, saying AYO was a brainwashing program, where they teach you to think just like them." He began to feel like an outsider because he didn't see each issue as black or white. Finally, Ryan made the difficult decision to leave AYO because they did "not allow for a variety of opinions."

So often, adolescents feel stuck in organizations or groups where they feel uncomfortable, but stay the course because of peer pressure or other influences. It impressed me that Ryan's reflection process led him to discern important meaning for himself and take action to leave the group. So I asked him how he learned to understand himself so well and if he could describe his reflection process in greater detail. Not surprisingly, he shared a story of how a single teacher had profoundly influenced his ability to self-reflect.

"I had a chorus teacher named Mr. Moore," Ryan said. "He was a Caucasian in his forties." Explaining that Mr. Moore had once given the class a writing assignment, Ryan quietly admitted, "I wrote something for him that he thought was very good." As they discussed Ryan's creative writing skills, "He encouraged me to keep writing to channel my emotions into some form of media, rather than keeping it bottled inside of me and being upset about things." He suggested to Ryan that he "could channel things into writing and let other people read it. It would help me with my ability to process my thoughts."

Ryan took Mr. Moore's advice, confessing, "He was the reason I got into writing poetry and rap songs. It was all him." Looking back, Ryan positively attributes AYO for changing his life. Not only did this group help him develop his identity as an Asian–American young man, but the struggle to come to terms with the organization's values was transformative for him.

Ryan's foray into creative writing evolved into a deep connection with all forms of artistic expression. Linking his ability to self-reflect with his engagement in the arts, he said, "When you make art, it's a form of expression. You form your own opinions about things." Ryan struggled for the right words to describe the self-reflection process, yet he knew it was implicit in how he expressed himself through his music and writing. "Expression and empowerment," he said, "go hand in hand."

As I watched Ryan perform his rap songs on a YouTube video he shared with me, his words about reflection and expression came to life on the stage. Full of energy and rhythm, he had found a perfect vehicle for expressing his thoughts and feelings. At the same time, he stayed true to the person who didn't like direct confrontation. "With art," Ryan said, "you can deliver a message and not be confrontational. People appreciate artwork and get the idea of what you're trying to say."

The Role of Challenge and Struggle

Ryan's story underscores the complexity and unpredictability of transformative learning. It reminds us that youth programs, no matter how well developed or intentioned, produce different outcomes for different young people. What remain important in all these stories are the underlying abilities that adolescents utilize to overcome challenges, and the quality of their relationship with adult mentors who guide them along the way.

While our greatest desire as parents and educators is for children to experience happiness, we know that the most meaningful learning is achieved when they reflect on moments of challenge and struggle. Whether struggle came from witnessing other people's suffering as Ashley described, from hard physical labor like Ryan's, or from battling one's innermost emotions like those found in the stories shared by Jared and Ryan, the message that struggle is intricately tied to meaning was repeated time and time again by the young people I interviewed.

Research studies have helped us understand that all young people must struggle in some way to achieve an identity that engages them as members of society. If they don't have experiences that challenge their values and moral character, they are less likely to develop the inner strengths and abilities they need to engage with meaningful life goals. The students I talked with dealt with moral dilemmas by turning inward to discover more about themselves and their worlds through self-reflection, an ability that has been consistently correlated with engaged young people (Colby & Sullivan, 2009). Scaffolded by adult mentors, they found encouragement, support, and acceptance through non-judgmental adult relationships that allowed them to openly share their thoughts and feelings.

Both psychology and neuroscience research have found self-reflection critical to the process of learning and developing purpose (Damon, 2008; Siegel, 2013). Yet self-reflection is vaguely defined, difficult to capture in words, and almost impossible to measure. Almost 100 years ago, John Dewey provided some of the best thinking about reflection (Dewey, 1933). Distilling important aspects of his insights on the reflective process, these three criteria help us understand its importance to youth development:

1. Reflection is a meaning-making process that helps young

people achieve deeper levels of understanding from their relationships and experiences.

2. Reflection happens with the help of community, through interaction with supportive adults.

3. Reflection deepens a desire to learn and grow.

Encouraging students to reflect on their life and volunteer service was part of the interview phase of my study with civically-engaged youth. But it was apparent that these young people had not only thought deeply about their volunteer experiences, but also about other critical events in their lives. Like Ryan, each spoke of adult mentors as playing key roles in supporting their reflection processes. As adults listened, encouraged, and supported, the most effective ones were very intentional about keeping ownership of the outcomes with the youth themselves. In other words, they didn't impose their own views on students.

INTEGRATING PERSPECTIVES

Rasheeda, a college senior at Adelphi University in New York, described a youth conference she attended in high school as the "emotional experience" that defined her as a "strong individual." Rasheeda said, "I became more outspoken and 'out there,' in the sense that I'm not afraid to speak my mind and fight for what I believe."

Born in Kabul, Afghanistan, Rasheeda's Muslim family immigrated to the U.S. as the result of war when she was just an infant. With successful careers and a comfortable lifestyle, her parents remained close to their Afghan roots, using whatever resources they could to help advocate for those in their native country. In addition to instilling a cultural awareness, Rasheeda's mother always reminded her that "it was our obligation to give back." She remembers times such as on her eighth birthday when she raised money and "sent it to earthquake victims instead of having a birthday party."

Like other families in this book, Rasheeda's parents helped set the stage for how she might respond when faced with difficult moral challenges as a teenager. But the inner work of adolescence goes beyond understanding childhood "obligation" to greater societal awareness. This shift happened for Rasheeda in high school when she was invited to attend an eight-day youth conference sponsored by a global nonprofit organization. The event took place, not half way around the world, but at a college near her hometown. "We were exposed to issues like HIV/AIDS, hunger, and poverty," Rasheeda said. "It was really a very life-changing experience for me."

Wanting to dig deeper into what initiated her deep learning, I asked Rasheeda if she could recall a critical moment or event during the conference that triggered a change inside her. Without hesitation, she told me about the impact of a music video that "brought half of the room of 50 students to tears," including her. The video, by Sarah McLaughlin, was called "World on Fire." Readily available on YouTube, the video cost McLaughlin only $15 to make, showing viewers the power that small actions have to improve the lives of people who are suffering.

"I was overwhelmed with all the information we had just learned during the first three days of the conference," Rasheeda admitted. "And then, to be shown this video—something through the form of art and a visual—made everything so clear." Describing her reaction like "turning on a switch," she then spoke intensely about how she began to process the "emotional aspect of being human."

Rasheeda attributed her path toward social activism to her experiences at the youth conference. But she also acknowledged "my family and cultural background, the groups I've been involved with, and the people I've met throughout my life" contributed to the role she now plays as a global change agent. In fact, how she found meaning through McLaughlin's video was facilitated by the same process as the other young people in this book.

Discovering Aha Moments

Rasheeda's experience illustrates the fourth stage in the transformative learning process—shifting perspectives. While many can recall an initial "aha moment" or the feeling of a light bulb going on in their heads, perspective change requires deep understanding gained through reflection and critical thinking. Not only does it involve how we view ourselves and our relationships, but it often changes our ideas about peace, education, humanity, and social justice (Morrell & O'Connor, 2002).

As you've likely recognized through the stories in this book, the experiences that cause adolescents to connect at boundaries, confront values, reflect on meaning, and change perspectives varies widely. Why is it important for adolescents to change perspectives? If they have been raised with positive values, like honesty, compassion, and kindness, aren't those values already a part of their inner identities?

These questions don't have easy answers, but brain science is helping us better understand why teenagers must struggle with these challenges. In his book, Brainstorm: The Power and Purpose of the Teenage Brain, Dan Siegel explains a concept he calls mindsight. Referring to the ability to really know our own minds, mindsight includes empathy, insight, and integration. The prefrontal cortex of the brain makes maps of our minds that help us sense other people's feelings (empathy), explore our own feelings (insight), and then merge them into an interconnected whole (integration). During the teen years, our brains learn to make these maps in new ways (Siegel, 2013).

While it is more likely that children raised with positive values will choose those values as teenagers, adolescence is a time when youth fully examine the values learned from childhood, draw meaning from them, and form an identity separate from their parents. Often, they reject some of their parents' beliefs while embracing others. Think of it as the brain's rite of passage to adulthood.

To demonstrate this process, remember back to when you were a child and your parents told you not to touch the hot stove. You probably followed their guidance because they instilled the fear that getting burned was very painful. But then one day you accidentally burned yourself. You came face-to-face with your own experience of pain—you understood pain differently.

While many volunteer or service-learning programs attempt to structure experiences that can be transformative for young people, this kind of learning often happens in unexpected ways. Similar to the physical learning involved with getting burned, transformative learning allows youth to draw on the internal values gleaned from families and educators during childhood and understand them differently. The understanding gained during these shifts in perspective often drive young people's direction and life purpose. Their perspective shifts are simply the brain's way of integrating what they know about others with what they know about themselves.

In Rasheeda's case, the young people at her youth conference were likely a lot like her—potential leaders of social change. And even though they shared many interests, it was not until they came together in a "different world" that they were pushed to confront their values and see other people's perspectives. Thus, transformation can occur when young people come together in a variety of challenging environments, including thought-provoking conferences, demanding outdoor group activities, and specialty summer camps. In fact, anytime a young person is pushed out of their comfort zone to tackle challenging, value-laden dilemmas, there is potential for learning that leads to higher levels of empathy, caring, and compassion.

LIVING AND LEADING WITH EMPATHY

Rasheeda's story takes us to the last stage of the transformative process, where empathy fuels action in the world. As mentioned earlier, the connection between internal learning and external action has been supported by many studies. For the young people in this book, they discovered ways to transfer what they had learned about themselves to causes in which they believed. They also became more open to other people's viewpoints and saw self-reflection as a positive source of internal strength.

Rasheeda planned to become a dentist and was immersed in coursework that would further her chosen career. She was also a "global scholar" at her college, committed to providing quality access to education for everyone. "With a little awareness and action," she said, "we can have more people going to school throughout the world." Rasheeda was particularly involved in helping Afghan women and children. "If you can educate a woman, you are in fact, creating impact on a larger scale."

Looking back on the people and experiences that helped her develop her own identity as an Afghan-American woman, Rasheeda spoke willfully, saying, "I'm working hard for the rights of women who seem to be vulnerable, but, in fact, are very strong." Through her authoritative voice and determined words, I could vividly sense her journey from an impressionable child to a compelling force for social change. I believed she would change the world, and so did she.

Like other young people I interviewed, Rasheeda expressed profound gratitude, particularly for the youth conference that was critical to her perspective shift and "call to action." As other students described, a sense of gratitude was common to these young people as they engaged themselves in efforts to "pay it forward." Transformative learning, therefore, became a process that produced many developmental benefits for teens, including the development of empathy, curiosity, sociability, resilience, self-awareness, integrity, resourcefulness, and creativity. Research shows these abilities lead to an engaged, fulfilling life.

TEEN BRAINS ARE READY FOR THE CHALLENGE

One of the complaints voiced by youth in my study was that adults often underestimated or undervalued students' abilities. Adolescents want to be innovators, inventors, and collaborators. But rather than looking at our relationships with teens as opportunities to connect at the edges of our own comfort zones, we look down on them, assuming they are not quite ready for full engagement. The truth is that teenagers are ready to be leaders and innovators. They are ready to learn from significant life challenges. Yet, they are stuck in a world that protects them and limits their development.

Research in cognitive neuroscience supports the notion that teenagers can experience transformative learning in much the same way as adults. Not only is the transition from childhood to adulthood characterized by dramatic changes in identity, it is also a time of increased cognitive flexibility (Rutter & Rutter, 1993). There is a measurable shift in how adolescents think, making them more self-aware and self-reflective than younger children. They develop the ability to understand multidimensional concepts and think in strategic ways (Blakemore & Choudhury, 2006). Brain research also dismisses the stereotype of adolescents as irrational risk-takers and shows that the logical-reasoning abilities of 15-year-olds are similar to those of adults (Steinberg, 2007). These cognitive abilities are key elements of empathy development and transformative learning during adolescence.

That said, it is important to acknowledge that the adolescent brain is different than the adult brain, and its changes are among the most dramatic to occur during the human lifespan. Scientists believe brain maturation in adolescence unfolds as a result of a teen's environment and experiences (Steinberg, 2010). Young people in my study showed that important skills were nurtured in environments that contained specific types of adult support. With these skills and abilities, teens had the kinds of learning experiences that increased their potential to be driven by empathy, compassion, kindness, and integrity—foundational for becoming innovators of social change.

SEVEN HABITS OF NURTURING ADULTS

As Millennials shared stories of how they turned empathy into civic action, it was clear they looked to the adults in their lives for support and encouragement. In fact, throughout their interviews, seven adult habits emerged as essential to young people's development as engaged citizens. These habits fostered the transformative learning process, helping youth connect with people different from themselves, confront their values, reflect on meaning, integrate their perspectives, and lead with empathy.

1. Notice When Teens Feel Challenged

The greatest potential for deep learning about empathy exists as teens struggle to overcome challenges. We are most helpful when we foster their courage, helping them to live and learn at the edge of their comfort zones. We do this by noticing when they are worried, frustrated, or angry, and then inviting them into conversations that acknowledge their feelings.

2. Encourage Positive Risk-taking

Adolescents naturally seek risk, challenge, and emotional stimulation. When we urge them to find meaning through community service rather than merely building resumes for college, we help young people engage in positive risk-taking, pushing their emotional boundaries and expanding their learning, creativity, and problem-solving skills.

3. Recognize and Value Unique Interests

Young people have interests that often go unnoticed or undervalued because they don't neatly fit into their structured school days. We help these interests blossom into seeds of transformative learning when we take time to get to know students outside of academics and connect them with new opportunities that feed their passions.

4. Support Creative Approaches to Expression

Developing the ability to care about others requires the ability to reflect and critically think about ourselves and the world around us. When we encourage teens to use multiple forms of expression, like creative writing, art, music, video, photography, and new digital mediums, we enable them to think and express ideas on a variety of complex issues.

5. Help Make Connections

Young people learn empathy when they connect with people who are different from them. When we connect youth with people who are struggling, have different lifestyles, or less privilege, we help them define their own identities. These opportunities can be found through connections in our own communities and also abroad in developing countries.

6. Stand Alongside

After-school programs, youth conferences, study abroad experiences, and volunteer organizations impact young people in different ways—both positive and negative. When we stand alongside youth and support them as they naturally struggle to process these experiences, we help them learn to live and lead with empathy.

7. Invite Deep Conversations

Adolescence is a time of discernment when young people draw meaning from the varied relationships and experiences they have encountered during their lifetimes. Rather than imposing values on teens, young people need us to actively listen, challenge them to think critically, and invite them to engage in thought-provoking dialogue.

6

The Roots of Thriving

We have to recognize that human flourishing is not a mechanical process; it's an organic process. And you cannot predict the outcome of human development. All you can do, like a farmer, is create the conditions under which they [children] will begin to flourish.

— Sir Ken Robinson, *Bring on the Learning Revolution*
TED Talk, 2010

When we view learning as a collection of individual parts, it is easy to think that educating and raising children to become engaged citizens evolves mainly from teaching them about citizenship, service, and the workings of democracy. While these are clearly important tasks, this thinking can also reduce citizenship into a less powerful phenomenon. It is only when we closely examine the life stories of children who emerged as participatory and justice-oriented citizens that we discover the conditions under which they began to thrive. Creating those conditions should be the goal of all families, schools, and communities who dream of a better future for all children.

From the stories in previous chapters, it is clear that a variety of meaningful service experiences provided young people with important developmental benefits. What the stories also suggest is that children flourish in life when they have the kind of positive relationships described by the engaged young citizens in this study. Those relationships with supportive parents, teachers, and mentors attended to the roots of their development, enabling young people to grow into the empathetic and committed citizens they became. This careful nurturing allowed adolescents to gain self-efficacy—a belief in one's capability to accomplish goals.

All youth need supportive adult relationships—people who believe in them and their potential. When young people engage with such adults, they learn to believe in themselves. Quite simply, that self-belief is one of the most important determinants of a young person's positive development and life success. It is also an essential component of individual and civic agency (Bandura, 2001). As it turns out, all of the young people in my study had internalized this self-belief and had put that belief to work in their quests to make the world a better place.

Youth especially attributed their success as social and environmental change makers to how adult mentors supported and influenced them during their high school years. Broadly speaking, these mentors included teachers, coaches, counselors, ministers, business leaders, youth program staff, and other caring adults. While most were non-parent mentors and role models, it is important to note that parents often played mentoring roles, particularly those parents who understood the changing needs of adolescents. Young people strongly conveyed that their adult mentors played a determining role in how they, as teenagers, felt about and motivated themselves. Their self-beliefs not only fostered civic engagement, but also helped them positively engage in all aspects of school, life, and work.

Describing a mentor who had lost his daughter to a school gang-related incident, Kaitlyn, then a high school sophomore, said, "He's been very helpful in opening up my eyes . . . and helping me learn more about me . . . how I can do it by myself and not rely on having to get [others] to help me."

Carlos talked about his high school guidance counselor and science teacher, two mentors who quite literally changed his life: "They helped me so much. I think basically everything I did was because of them. . . . They were always pushing me." Carlos paused to reflect, and then continued, "What I learned from them was if you have a problem it's always good to share it with somebody because they might see the problem in a different way."

Whoever these powerful mentors were, they played a quiet but profound role in young people's lives. For example, Danielle highlighted this kind of advocacy when she spoke of an older cousin who mentored her:

> One of the things he does best is listening. I can remember going over to visit and we would go four-wheeling or just stand out on the porch and look at the stars at night and he could tell something was on my mind. He was always able to read my face and then ask what was on my mind. He would just let me talk it out. And then he wouldn't try to tell me what to do or what he thought was appropriate. He would instead just be thoughtful and quiet and then he would remind me who I was. . . . He showed that he had faith in me and he knew that I would make a good choice.

COMING-OF-AGE STORIES

Mentoring was not the primary focus of my original research with civically-engaged youth; yet I came to understand its importance from listening to young people who told me about adults who changed their lives. When I realized that *all* of the youth in my study could point to these mentors during their teen years, I knew I needed to investigate this phenomenon further.

Many formal mentoring programs exist today to support teenagers, and for good reason. Adolescence is a time when youth "come of age"—when they search for a sense of identity that includes a belief they can accomplish their chosen goals. That self-belief touches every aspect of young people's lives, and determines whether they emerge as motivated, productive, and optimistic young adults (Pajares & Urdan, 2006).

Each of the young people in this book shared coming-of-age stories—narratives that helped define their civic identities. But many kinds of stories help illuminate the journey through adolescence and the important role the teen years play in a young person's life. *The Wizard of Oz* is an iconic story that has lived in the hearts of millions of people around the world. If it were simply a story of a young girl as she meandered down a yellow brick road to meet a wizard, we would likely have forgotten about it decades ago. But Dorothy's journey was a powerful coming-of-age story, similar to the stories told by young people in my study.

Dorothy, an orphaned teenager who lived on a Kansas farm with her aunt and uncle, daydreamed about going "over the rainbow." Along the road to find the Wizard, she encountered three characters who became her friends and mentors:

1. The Scarecrow who wanted a brain
2. The Tin Man who longed for a heart
3. The Cowardly Lion who wished for courage

On her journey, she was hindered by the Wicked Witch who deluged Dorothy and her friends with one challenge after another. The civically-engaged youth in my study overcame many challenges too.

In fact, since *The Wizard of Oz* was written, a whole new field of neuroscience has shed light on the importance of these challenges. What we've learned from the research in neuroscience is that teen brains crave risk, challenge, and emotional stimulation. Those drives are a natural part of adolescence and they were critical to both Dorothy's story and to the stories of the young people in this book.

In an article, "What Happy People Do Differently," positive psychologists Robert Biswas-Diener and Todd Kashdan (2013) claimed that truly happy people understand "happiness is not just about doing things that you like. It also requires growth and adventuring beyond the boundaries of your comfort zone." They suggest, "Curiosity is largely about exploration . . . the most direct route to becoming stronger and wiser." A study led by Kashdan and Steger (2007) found that "curious people invest in activities that cause them discomfort as a springboard to higher psychological peaks."

Changes to the limbic system of the brain cause teens to seek risk, challenge, and emotional stimulation. While some parents fear this phase of a child's life, it is a natural and often positive transition to adulthood. These normal, neurological drives are why teens like being pushed out of their comfort zones. At the peak of some of their most challenging experiences, the young people in my study said:

"I crossed barriers in my mind."

"I felt scared."

"I felt liberated."

"What a powerful experience."

"I was way out of my comfort zone."

What kind of experiences caused them to make these comments? At first glance, it might sound like they were high on drugs or alcohol.

But it was quite the opposite. These young people were describing the positive experience of pushing their psychological boundaries as they participated in a variety of community service activities. Some had come face-to-face with people living in situations very different from their own, like poverty or homelessness. Others were doing physical labor that stretched them to new levels of endurance. Several feared failure as they set their sights on unimaginable goals to benefit others.

What these young people showed was that teens can get the stimulation their brains require through much more positive means than what we usually associate with adolescent risk-taking. For example, in my study, risk-taking was associated with such things as mountain climbing, community service, politics, faith groups, and other experiences that make youth uncomfortable, but reward them handsomely. When they learn to overcome real challenges in the real world, they begin to use their brains to find meaning, they discover what's inside their hearts, and they find courage to persevere despite life's obstacles.

We must begin to question the idea that teen risk-taking is always negative and look for ways that adult mentors support young people through the psychological challenges associated with adolescence. Like the Scarecrow, the Tin Man, and the Lion, mentors must be supportive listeners, active problem-solvers, and people who help teens believe in themselves.

When Dorothy finally encountered the Wizard, she was deeply disappointed. Why? Because she believed that wisdom was *outside* of herself and *inside* of someone else. She looked to the Wizard for wisdom. But Glinda, the Good Witch, gave Dorothy the greatest gift of all—the knowledge that she always had the power within herself to get back to Kansas anytime she wanted. And indeed, Dorothy began to believe in herself and her own abilities.

Simply stated, this is the adolescent story. And it's a story that we should want for all teens. One of the main reasons why schools and after-school programs enrich young people's lives is because they enable youth to connect to wise mentors. Like the Scarecrow, the Tin Man, and the Lion, mentors counsel and support young people in a manner that facilitates growth and learning. They don't pretend to have the answers, unlike the Wizard. Instead, they try to draw out what already exists inside each young person.

These are the same qualities that the young people in my study described when they talked about their mentors. What made these youth thrive, not just as citizens, but as extraordinary human beings, had nothing to do with grade point averages, test scores, or which colleges they attended. It had everything to do with how they found meaning, purpose, and wisdom in the world. No movie depicts this message better than *The Wizard of Oz*.

THE POWER OF MENTORING ADOLESCENTS

Even though our understanding of positive youth development has grown considerably over the past decade, the effectiveness of many mentoring programs remains in question (DuBois et al., 2011). One reason lies in the quality of adult–youth relationships and how adults view their mentoring roles. In recent years, youth mentoring has begun to evolve from a process focused on correcting youth problems to developing young people's internal strengths, much like the focus of Dorothy's mentors in *The Wizard of Oz*. The latter is a practice that helps youth recognize and understand their abilities in ways that enable them to make a difference for themselves and their communities (Liang et al., 2013). This shift occurs when mentors stop seeing themselves merely as teachers, advisors, and role models, and start seeing themselves as listeners, encouragers, supporters, and co-learners.

This more "thoughtful and quiet" relationship, like the one Danielle described, elevates learning for mentors and mentees. It is respectful and compassionate, helping youth gain a deeper belief in self and chart meaningful pathways through school and life. The highly engaged youth in my study claimed that these quiet advocates were transformative to their personal growth and career development. They helped them learn to thrive in an increasingly complex and confusing world.

Mentoring is critical to positive youth development. One of the largest mentoring studies ever conducted continues to support this thinking and also links mentoring to a reduction in bullying. The five-year study sponsored by the Centre for Addiction and Mental Health (2013) and Big Brothers Big Sisters Canada found that children with mentors were more confident and had fewer behavioral problems. Girls in the study were four times less likely to become bullies than those without a mentor, and boys were two times less likely. In general, young people showed increased belief in their abilities to succeed in school and felt less anxiety related to peer pressure.

Mentoring relationships with youth are complicated and there is more to be learned about what makes them succeed, particularly when mentors are matched through organizations like Big Brothers Big Sisters and other nonprofits. In my research with teens who became engaged citizens, all of the young people in the study had naturally developed mentee-mentor relationships with adults sometime during their middle and high school years. None were matched by organizations. Non-parent mentors— teachers, clergy, and civic leaders—were highly instrumental in how these teens learned to believe in themselves and tackle challenging goals—much like those in the Big Brothers Big Sisters study.

It is clear that disadvantaged teens receive a significant benefit from mentoring. A study conducted by North Carolina State University

(2009) showed that youth from disadvantaged backgrounds are twice as likely to attend college when they have a mentor, particularly a teacher. It also showed that less than half of disadvantaged students have any adult mentor and that only seven percent named a teacher as a mentor. In contrast, all of the civically-engaged youth in my study named teachers as mentors.

A study of African American youth showed how important mentors were to teens with hardships (Kogan et al., 2011). For example, young people who had experienced discrimination, family stress, or abuse were less likely to break the law or engage in substance abuse if they had a positive mentoring relationship. Again, their mentors provided the relational support to help them believe in their abilities and overcome difficult life challenges.

While many studies have focused on the effects of mentoring disadvantaged teens, my study showed that all teens reap big developmental dividends from mentoring relationships during their middle and high school years. Teens grew intellectually, interpersonally, and emotionally from their relationships with supportive adults whether young people grew up in affluent, middle income, or disadvantaged families.

QUALITIES OF EXCEPTIONAL MENTORS

Most studies have focused on the effects of mentorship on youth rather than what adults actually do in their roles as mentors. In my interviews with young people, I asked for more specific information about these relationships. In particular, I wanted to know what made adults exceptional mentors, helping youth grow and develop in ways young people themselves viewed as beneficial. Consequently, common themes emerged about the the ways mentors support youth.

Young people agreed that adults are more likely to influence their life paths if they possess the following qualities, first outlined in Chapter 4 with supporting quotes from youth. The qualities are expanded and summarized below, indicating that exceptional mentors are:

1. Supportive and Encouraging

By far, the most important role of a mentor, according to the young people in this book, is to support and encourage them, particularly as they struggle to overcome obstacles and solve problems. When young people feel depressed, upset with their families, or unhappy in their life situations, mentors stand beside them, letting them talk about anything and reminding them of their innate value as human beings.

2. Active Listeners

Mentors listen first and speak last. Many teens mentioned how little they feel listened to by most adults. Often, they feel inferior even when they have good ideas. But mentors are different. They always listen, even when they are not obligated to do so.

3. People Who Push—Just Enough

As parents can attest, most teens don't respond well to being pushed out of their comfort zones, particularly within their families. But teens like to have high expectations set for them—both academically and personally. They appreciate when mentors push them beyond what they may have imagined they could accomplish. In fact, this is likely the reason why mentored youth from disadvantaged backgrounds are twice as likely to attend college.

4. Authentically Interested in Youth as Individuals

The teens who shared their stories with me acknowledged that they can tell the difference between adults who are authentically interested in them as individuals and those who are just playing a role. Mentors engage youth to understand all aspects of their lives and interests. They value young people's ideas and honor their changing feelings and moods.

5. *Nurturers of Self Decision-Making*

Good mentors don't judge young people or impose their own beliefs on them. Instead, young people say they remind them who they are and help them believe they have the insights to make good choices. Knowing they are not being judged helps young people think through decisions critically, sifting through the deeper values that will inform the adults they become.

6. *Sources of Perspective*

Adult mentors provide perspective to young people from their additional years of life experience. When obstacles seem overwhelming, mentors help put those challenges in perspective. They also help young people see both sides of a situation, helping model the skills of positive skepticism.

PROSPERING IN A COMPLEX WORLD

A key question for youth mentors is "What does human flourishing look like for children in today's society?" It is impossible to deny the complexity of modern society and the challenges youth face as a result of growing up in a thornier, multifaceted world. Scientific, technological, and cultural advances have brought better quality of life, greater freedoms, and detailed levels of specialization that have benefited millions of people.

Civic change makers of the past several decades have alleviated hunger, reduced racism, and responded to social and environmental injustices around the globe. Yet as leaders and innovators have helped solve many problems, they have also created others for future generations to solve. For many, those problems are more complex and deeply rooted in cultural, political, and ethical contradictions.

It is not surprising then, that the young people who shared their stories with me were highly skeptical of mentors who encouraged them to think in rigid ways or to impose value-laden expectations on them. Intuitively, they understood that complexity required greater flexibility and that ideological polarization reduced the potential of collaborative outcomes for positive change.

It is time to merge what we know about child development with the science of complexity on behalf of a new generation. Scientists who have studied complexity in physical, biological, and social systems over decades have made important discoveries. Through analysis of how animals, people, organizations, and communities prosper in the real world, scientists have unlocked keys to understanding how success emerges in an age of increasing complexity. Their insights have transformed many businesses and organizations, helping managers understand that success is more closely linked to broad patterns and principles than to narrowly restrictive measurement systems.

These findings are often contrary to the way we naturally think as educators, parents, youth mentors, and policy makers. Key ideas from complexity science include:

1. We cannot explain or alter complex systems by reducing them into ever-finer detail.
2. The core principles that lead toward success and thriving are relatively simple.
3. Small changes in patterns and relationships produce large effects.

How do these basic scientific concepts help us rethink what success and prospering looks like for current and future generations of children and how we educate, mentor, and parent them? Today, we have come to believe that the right recipe for raising children is in the finer details of specialized learning. For example, if we want to raise innovative civic change makers, we teach kids about citizenship, social entrepreneurship, government, leadership, and social change strategies. If we want them to get accepted into a good college, we make sure they have the right mix of achievements and experiences on their resumes.

This thinking seems logical, but goes against what we know about both complexity and child development. It is not the detailed achievements that help kids thrive in an emerging world of growing complexity. Success and happiness are driven by a much simpler set of principles and patterns of behavior. When those behaviors are reinforced through supportive adult relationships, children gain big developmental advantages. The young people in my study told story after story that reinforced this thinking.

In the sections that follow, I outline eight core abilities that each young person in this book developed as a result of their connections with supportive adults. The service experiences that gave young people opportunities for personal growth were *relational experiences*—experiences intricately tied to human interaction. When mentors came into young people's lives, they helped foster the conditions by which these youth learned to thrive.

To better articulate this set of core abilities, I drew insight from youth who often spoke of emotional struggles to find themselves—to discover their own *internal compasses*. Most agreed that their struggles were positively facilitated by mentors, like the youth worker that Scott described who "didn't impose her beliefs on me. She just would lead me to my own answers. . . . I felt like I was talking to a friend who knew just a little more than me."

As I listened intently to young people tell stories about their relationships with adult mentors, it was clear that what they had gained developmentally enabled them to accomplish their goals. In this particular study, those goals were related to improving society. But do these same developmental benefits help young people achieve whatever goals they set out to accomplish in life? And if so, how do we instill these core abilities in all young people?

For the past several years, I have pursued the answers to these questions through synthesizing research in a variety of multidisciplinary fields. My goal was to identify and articulate a framework that depicted the abilities that not only led my study participants to thrive as civically-engaged young people, but may also shed light on the roots of thriving for all children.

THE COMPASS ADVANTAGE: A TOOL FOR GUIDING YOUTH

Evolved from the stories in this book, *The Compass Advantage* ™ is an organizing framework for understanding how parents, schools, and communities support young people on their paths toward fulfilling lives. At its foundation are eight core abilities known to propel children's success in complex times, wherever their career paths may lead. The stories and insights that young people shared about how their relationships and experiences helped them develop these core abilities support decades of research by experts in the fields of education, child development, leadership, complexity science, psychology, and neuroscience.

Using key concepts from our understanding of how humans thrive in a more complicated, highly specialized world, the framework is purposely simplistic. Educators, parents, nonprofit and civic leaders, after-school program staff, and policy makers should recognize how their work with youth influences the compass abilities. Collectively, adults impact how young people develop internal compasses—guidance systems that give children the capacity to grow into caring, capable, and engaged adults. With a compass to point the way, youth learn to successfully chart their own meaningful lives. They become flexible, adaptable, open-minded, and collaborative individuals, ready to tackle whatever lies ahead. It's a simple yet powerful lens in which to view positive youth development and the roles all adults play in supporting young people.

In the sections that follow, each of these core abilities is described in greater detail. Young people's stories illustrate how adults nurture these abilities in many different contexts. While this chapter primarily focuses on adolescence, these abilities are fostered by supportive adults throughout a child's growing-up years. For articles that further expand on how these abilities are influenced by parents, teachers, and mentors during the K-12 school years, readers are invited to visit *RootsOfAction.com,* a website dedicated to applying the principles of

The Compass Advantage™ in homes, schools, and after-school environments.

CURIOSITY: THE HEART OF LIFELONG LEARNING

What makes children *want* to learn about the world around them? According to research, it's the joy of exploration—a hidden force that drives learning, critical thinking, and reasoning. We call this ability *curiosity* and it helps children seek and acquire new knowledge, skills, and ways of understanding the world. It is at the heart of what motivates young people to learn and what keeps them learning throughout their lives. We recognize curiosity in children when we see them exploring their environment, devouring books and information, asking questions, investigating concepts, manipulating data, searching for meaning, connecting with people and nature, and seeking new learning experiences.

Most parents and educators understand that curiosity supercharges learning in the classroom. But they also know that many children can achieve good grades *without* being curious—by understanding the system of test-taking and dutifully doing their homework. Curious children may spend a great deal of time reading and acquiring knowledge because they sense a gap between what they know and what they want to know—not because they are motivated by grades.

When kids are in curiosity's grip, they often forget the immediate goals at hand because they are preoccupied with learning. This was clearly the case with many young people who shared their stories with me. Some were so focused on learning how to mobilize efforts around a particular civic issue or understand the root causes of a social problem, that they missed school deadlines or didn't have time to study for an exam. They defined their success differently than many of today's youth. They wanted to learn, not just achieve good grades.

Research suggests intellectual curiosity has as big of an effect on performance as hard work (von Stumm et al., 2011). In fact, one attribute that helps young people thrive in the workplace is their *openness to experience*, which involves being curious and open-minded (Sackett & Walmsley, 2014). When combined, curiosity and hard work account for success just as much as intelligence. Gruber (2014) found that people who were curious about a topic retained what they learned for longer periods of time. And even more impressive, curiosity has been linked to a wide range of important adaptive behaviors, including tolerance of anxiety and uncertainty, positive emotions, humor, playfulness, out-of-box thinking, and a noncritical attitude—all attributes associated with healthy social outcomes in an ever-increasingly complex society (Kashdan et al., 2013).

Jacqueline's Story

Supportive adults help youth understand the tenets of engaged learning when they recognize the different ways youth explore—by touching, feeling, tasting, climbing, smelling, etc.—and praise them for their perseverance to find answers. When mentors show young people how parts connect and influence the whole of society, youth discover that curiosity improves relationships, fuels innovation, and drives social change.

When Jacqueline was in high school, she discovered an interest in education and child welfare. With the help of mentors, she became curious about politics and how government influenced the issues that mattered most to her. She was drawn to the Republican Party through Barry Goldwater's philosophy in *The Conscience of a Conservative* and was inspired by a number of leaders in the GOP. But it was a small handful of high school teachers and after-school program advisors that inspired her to explore her interests further.

Jacqueline described her mentors as "very passionate about their subjects and very passionate about what their students were doing related to those subjects." When she became involved in student council, she got to know Mr. Drew, the advisor of that program. "Mr. Drew," Jacqueline said, "was very committed to his students. If I ever had a problem, I could go to him."

Jacqueline was not unlike other young people who described how they were motivated in middle and high school to explore their interests. The key with all the youth in my study was their ability to connect with adults who stimulated their curiosity yet allowed them the freedom to find their own pathways to learning. For the most part, teachers and after-school program leaders played these roles. They modeled curiosity in their own lives and work. They accepted young people as individuals and made themselves available when youth needed an open ear or helping hand.

Rather than guiding teens to *right* answers, adults who mentored young people's curiosity helped them become skeptics. The term skeptic is derived from the Greek *skeptikos*, meaning "to inquire" or "to look around." Skeptics require additional evidence before accepting someone's claims as true. They are willing to challenge the status quo with open-minded, deep questioning. Galileo and Steve Jobs were skeptics. So was Jacqueline, whose questioning and curiosity about politics helped her become the student body vice president of a large university and plan a career in public service.

Mentors nurture curiosity when they encourage youth to identify and seek answers to questions that pique their interests in science, math, literature, civics, art, engineering, technology, and a myriad of other topics. When they help youth recognize failure as an opportunity for exploration, mentors encourage experimentation and new discovery. In turn, young people feel safe and inspired to explore their interests, ask questions, and make connections that are personally meaningful and fulfilling.

SOCIABILITY: THE CORE OF SOCIAL LEARNING AND WELLBEING

What helps children *engage* in learning? According to studies on the social nature of how we acquire knowledge, one answer is clear: Children engage in learning through their cooperative capacity to interact with others. We often call this *sociability,* and we recognize it in children when we observe their enjoyment of being together—chatting, joking, laughing, working, and creating friendships. It is through these interactions that kids make the invisible visible, cross boundaries into new spheres of learning, and initiate thoughts and feelings that help them chart pathways through life.

Key aspects of sociability are derived from skills that help children understand and express feelings and behaviors in ways that facilitate positive relationships and emotional wellbeing. In *The Compass Advantage*™, these interpersonal skills include self-regulation, active listening, cooperation, and effective communication. Sociability and its related skills are part of social and emotional learning (SEL), a field of study that has evolved in recent years to bring attention to and help train teachers and parents about these "softer" skills and their importance in education and child development. The five competencies most often associated with social emotional learning, include self-awareness, self-management, social awareness, relationship skills, and responsible decision making (Albright et al., 2011).

We don't have to look far for research that shows the benefits of sociability and how it is facilitated through positive adult-child relationships. For example, research by Jones, Bouffard and Weissbourd (2013) suggested that "teachers with stronger SEL competencies have more positive relationships with students, manage their classrooms more effectively, and implement SEL programs targeting to students with greater fidelity." They also claimed that supportive school cultures not only enhance the social competencies of adults who work there, but more importantly, provide the conditions under which children learn to develop positive interpersonal skills.

Social skills are developed in children through relational experiences both inside and outside of classrooms. These skills have been recognized by hundreds of social scientists whose research has linked sociability to positive development and wellbeing (Argyle 2013, Foschi & Lauriola 2014, Durlak et al., 2011). When children learn to work cooperatively with others, measurable benefits result, including reduced aggression, improved impulse control, and greater achievement in school.

Jennifer's Story

Adult mentors improve young people's sociability when they help youth understand that the words they choose make a difference to the relationships they create. When mentors help youth see that every social interaction is tied to an emotional reaction, young people learn to avoid impulsive behavior and think through difficult situations before acting.

When Jennifer was a junior in high school, she explained that Mrs. Dennard, a teacher, "taught me how to express my feelings." She went on to admit, "I'm a very thought-driven person and I don't like being emotionally vulnerable." She described a very stressful social situation that involved Nancy, a classmate whose personality was very different from Jennifer's. Coincidentally, Jennifer and Nancy ended up as officers on the same student council. During a particular interaction, Nancy ". . . reacted very strongly against me verbally and abusively, calling me names," said Jennifer, who felt devastated by this personal attack.

At Jennifer's invitation, Mrs. Dennard agreed to work with the two girls and even hold a mediation session between them. Jennifer admitted, "This was a very stressful experience because Nancy was someone I didn't want to work with again." In the end, Jennifer and Nancy learned to work through their differences. While they never became best friends, they began to understand themselves and each other in ways that contributed to their mutual work on the student council. As Jennifer reflected back, she said, "It was much easier for me to think, 'you're wrong and I'm right,'" but what she learned from working with Nancy for an entire academic year profoundly impacted her ability to work with others in the future. "This one experience," Jennifer said, "taught me to pay more attention to my emotions rather than just my thoughts."

Adults who mentor young people's development of sociability help them gain the capacity to work collaboratively with others to accomplish goals much bigger than themselves. Rather than enforcing rules and compliance, mentors who give youth a voice in creating their own shared social norms also help young people create the conditions that lead to cooperative behavior and increased learning. Jennifer's conflict resolution with a classmate in high school, aided by a perceptive and capable mentor, helped her move more confidently forward to college and beyond, where she has undertaken ambitious work to end sex trafficking and violence against women.

RESILIENCE: THE CAPACITY TO GROW FROM ADVERSITY

Over 100 years ago, the great African American educator Booker T. Washington spoke about *resilience* when he said, "I have learned that success is to be measured not so much by the position that one has reached in life as by the obstacles overcome while trying to succeed."

Research has since established resilience as essential for human thriving, and a critical ability for the development of healthy, adaptable young people. It's what enables children to *emerge* from challenging experiences with a positive sense of themselves and their futures. Children who develop resilience are better able to face disappointment, learn from failure, cope with loss, and adapt to change. We recognize resilience in children when we observe their determination, grit, and perseverance to tackle problems and cope with the emotional challenges of school and life.

Resilience is not a genetic trait. It is derived from the ways children learn to think and act when they are faced with obstacles, large and small. The road to resilience comes first and foremost from children's supportive relationships with parents, teachers, and other caring adults. These relationships become sources of strength when children work through stressful situations and painful emotions. When we help young people cultivate an approach to life that views obstacles as a critical part of success, we help them develop resilience.

Many parents and educators are familiar with Carol Dweck's (2006) research about growth mindsets—a way of thinking that helps children connect growth with hard work and perseverance. She discovered that praising children for how they tackle problems and rebound from adversity is much more effective for their growth as human beings than praising them for being smart or clever. Developing growth mindsets is a paradigm for children's life success, a way of helping them believe in themselves. It is often the greatest gift parents and teachers give to young people.

The ability to meet and overcome challenges in ways that maintain or promote well-being plays an essential role in how children learn to achieve academic and personal goals (Goldstein & Brooks, 2012). In the past, researchers who studied resilience devoted their attention to high-risk populations, particularly to children living in poverty. But because the 21st century has brought such complexity to all children's lives, the study of resilience has expanded significantly. No child is immune from the stressful, fast-paced environments in which they grow up, including youth from affluent communities (Luthar et al., 2013).

Brook's Story

Resilient young people feel a sense of control over their own destinies. They know they can reach out to others for support when needed, and they readily take initiative to solve problems. Adult mentors facilitate resilience by helping children think about and consider various paths through adversity. They also help by being supportive, encouraging self-awareness, and fostering self-decision making.

When Brook spoke about her family and mentors, she did so with a deep sense of gratefulness. "I grew up," she said, "under the proverb that it takes a village to raise a child. I started to develop a sense of how important a community is because I lived in one—a very strong and closely knit one." During her freshman year of high school, Brook's mother was diagnosed with cancer, putting a great deal of stress on her family. "I didn't want to allow my own worries and burdens to affect my family," she said, "so I started reaching out to several teachers. Mr. King and Mrs. Cartwright were very good listeners." They showed empathy and understanding for Brook's situation and listened as she tried to understand her feelings.

Later on, Brook's mother died and Brook's older sister detached from the family as she tried to cope with such a devastating loss. When Brook discovered a suicide note on her sister's door and realized she was missing, these same teachers showed up to support Brook. Both teachers worked together to locate resources to help find Brook's sister. Fortunately, the two sisters were reunited and were able to get the emotional support they needed. As Brook reflected on how these teachers helped her bounce back from adversity, she said, "I don't mean to sound hokey or idealistic, but I think the world really is a good place and that a lot of people are good people and will help if they can. They key," says Brook, "is giving people the chance to help by telling them what you need." These are wise words from a person of Brook's age and a message that all children should understand.

Adult mentors build resilience particularly when young people are at the edges of their intellectual, emotional, social, or physical comfort zones. When mentors support and encourage youth as they face adversity and overcome obstacles, young people learn how to rebuild and grow from life's challenges, big and small. Brooke went on to discover a passion for public education, particularly for underserved populations. In college, she helped found a chapter of Oxfam America on her campus.

SELF-AWARENESS: THE SOURCE OF MEANING AND PURPOSE

How do children gain a deeper understanding of how they think, feel, and act so they can improve their learning and develop meaningful relationships? Since the dawn of antiquity, philosophers have been intrigued with how human beings develop self-awareness—the ability to examine and understand who we are relative to the world around us. Today, scientists believe it is developed through skills like self-reflection, meaning-making, and the process of honing core values and beliefs. Self-awareness impacts young people's capacity to see themselves as uniquely different from other people.

Research not only shows that self-awareness evolves during childhood, but also that its development is linked to metacognitive processes of the brain. We know that if children reflect on how they learn, they become better learners. With greater awareness of how they acquire knowledge, young people learn to regulate their behavior to optimize learning. They begin to see how their strengths and weaknesses affect how they perform. As children's metacognitive abilities increase, research suggests they also achieve at higher levels (Weil et al., 2013).

Self-awareness, the inner source of how we glean meaning from life experiences, plays an important role in learning. Beyond academic learning, when young people gain awareness of their own mental states, they begin to answer important questions, including: How do I live a happy life? How do I become a respected human being? How do I develop hope and faith? Through these reflections, they also begin to understand other people's perspectives and feel empathy for larger groups of people.

Associated with the paralimbic network of the brain, scientists believe self-awareness serves as a "tool for monitoring and controlling our behavior and adjusting our beliefs of the world, not only within ourselves, but, importantly, between individuals" (Lou 2015). This higher-order thinking strategy actually changes the structure of the brain, making it more flexible and open to even greater learning.

Self-awareness plays a critical role in how children learn because it helps them become more efficient at focusing on what they still need to learn. The ability to reflect on and discover internal meaning increases with age, particularly from 12 years onward. This metacognitive skillfulness is thought to be a better predictor of learning than intelligence (Veenman & Spaans, 2005).

Samira's Story

When mentors cultivate children's abilities to reflect on, monitor, and evaluate their school and life experiences, young people become more self-reliant, flexible, and productive. Children improve their capacity to weigh choices and evaluate options, particularly when answers are not obvious. When children have difficulty understanding, they rely on reflective strategies to recognize their difficulties and attempt to rectify them. Improving metacognitive strategies provides young people with tools to reflect and grow in their emotional, intellectual, and social lives.

Born in China, Samira and her family moved to the U.S. when she was 10. The oldest child in a traditional Chinese family, Samira said, "I started feeling slighted when my first brother was born. I knew it was because I was a girl." Describing herself as "stubborn and outspoken," Samira fought back and often felt angry. She spoke of the history of female infanticide in China and how the "favoring of boys was still part of her culture." Growing up, Samira struggled to understand herself in light of feeling less cherished and loved than her brothers.

Samira sought out female role models. She saved newspaper articles about women she admired. She studied their stories and wanted to be like them. In high school, Samira became interested in aeronautics. Janet, a helicopter pilot, became one of her mentors. Janet gave Samira ground school lessons in flying and the two became friends. One of the many topics they discussed was gender discrimination in the civilian aviation industry. Samira began to see connections between various types of discrimination.

In her senior year of high school, Samira chose to explore gender discrimination in a year-long class project. "It was called QUEST," she said, "and it stood for question, understand, experience, service, and testimony." Mentored by a teacher as she explored her topic, Samira not only discovered a passion for helping others who felt victims of discrimination, but also became more aware of herself.

Mentors stimulate self-awareness in young people when they engage them in reflective conversations about values, beliefs, attitudes, and moral dilemmas. When mentors encourage youth to understand and attend to their intellectual, emotional, social, spiritual, and physical selves, they help young people understand the value of their full human potential. The project Samira undertook in high school was a perfect vehicle for her to struggle with her values and beliefs. "Knowing that certain adults were there alongside me and understood my feelings," said Samira, "was so important."

As a college student, Samira says she is "finding her voice." She reads books by female activists, including women who spoke out during the American Civil Rights Movement and those who have been refugees from places like Somalia and other countries that have oppressed women. She is a leader in several college groups, including Students for Global Citizenship and envisions a future helping empower women around the world.

INTEGRITY: THE BASIS OF SOCIAL HARMONY AND ACTION

As we seek to prepare young people with skills for career success, businessman and philanthropist Warren Buffet reminds us what makes great employees: "In looking for people to hire, look for three qualities: integrity, intelligence, and energy. And if they don't have the first one, the other two will kill you."

Integrity is about doing the right thing, even when no one is watching; and about courage, honesty, and respect in one's daily interactions. Unfortunately, we live in an age where "the end justifies the means" has become the mantra of far too many adults who are role models for children. Admittedly, the underlying issues that lead to dishonesty are often complex and multidimensional. People rationalize their actions with seemingly valid reasons. But as Buffet suggests, a lack of integrity comes with a high price tag.

How do children learn to be honest, respect societal norms, and act in ways consistent with the values, beliefs, and moral principles they claim to hold? How do parents, teachers and youth mentors instill and reinforce a code of ethics for children, particularly when research suggests the current culture of high-stakes testing fosters dishonesty (Anderman & Murdock, 2011)? These are tough questions with no simple answers.

Children are not born with integrity or the behaviors we associate with it, like honesty, honor, respect, authenticity, social responsibility, and the courage to stand up for what they believe is right. It is derived through a process of cultural socialization—influences from all spheres of a child's life. In their school environments, students acquire these values and behaviors from adult role models and peers, and in particular, through an understanding of the principles of academic integrity.

Most K–12 educators recognize that the students they teach today will become the leaders of tomorrow. Academic curriculum is constantly updated to meet the increasing demands of a changing knowledge society. Yet, we pay far less attention to the habits that build ethical leaders—habits that develop during childhood and adolescence. A recent study noted that 40% of U.S. faculty members have ignored cases of cheating in their courses, an indication that teachers don't want to "rock the boat" or deal with angry parents (Simha, 2014).

Integrity, and the moral and ethical principles we associate with it, is the basis of social harmony and action. Despite the many societal forces that test these principles daily, children deserve a world that values truth, honesty, and justice.

Giovanni's Story

Mentors help shape integrity by treating young people with respect and dignity, and listening to their feelings and concerns without judgment. When mentors praise youth for demonstrating their values, beliefs, and principles through actions, young people are reminded of their value as ethical human beings, beyond external achievements like grades or test scores.

Giovanni grew up in what he called "an extremely wealthy, racist, and overprotective family." The oldest of four boys, he recalled how isolated he felt and had no idea what was going on in the world around him. The irony, Giovanni said, was that his family had the resources to send him to an excellent religious middle and high school where he found teachers and mentors who listened to his ideas and thinking—ideas that were much different from his parents.

"I would have grown up to be just like my parents," Giovanni claimed. "But instead, I've learned to see the impact of the decisions I make on a broader scale." Rev. Andrew, a priest who became one of Giovanni's mentors listened and guided him in ways that helped Giovanni find his own identity, separate from his parents—an identity that included service to others and moral principles inherent in a just and caring society. It was through his non-judgmental acceptance of Giovanni that Rev. Andrew sparked this young man's curiosity in people who were different than himself, and gave Giovanni the confidence to stand for what he believed was morally and ethically right.

When I interviewed Giovanni, he was a senior in college and was very active in Campus Ministry. After graduation, he was moving to Burma where he planned to teach English and computer skills to Burmese children. His long term goal was to become a Jesuit priest, a career he hoped someday his family would accept.

Regardless of the families in which children are raised, all young people struggle with who they are as moral human beings during their adolescent years. Every student in my study—whether their parents were rich, poor, liberal, or conservation—faced similar dilemmas to find their "moral center." In each case, non-parent mentors played extraordinary roles as they allowed young people to assess what was "right" for them as individuals.

RESOURCEFULNESS: THE POWER TO SHAPE THE FUTURE

In the words of Tony Robbins, "Success is not about your resources. It's about how resourceful you are with what you have."

How do children learn to use knowledge to achieve goals? Unless information is processed, organized, and applied, knowledge can become a source of frustration rather than fulfillment. Children learn to use and apply knowledge as they gain skills in planning, organizing, decision-making, and problem-solving. Together, these skills are the building blocks of *resourcefulness*—the ability to find and use available resources to achieve goals. When young people imagine multiple outcomes, set objectives, experiment with new approaches, and negotiate challenges, they make important connections between knowledge and goal achievement. They become conscientious creators of their own futures.

High grades and test scores are not reliable indicators of resourcefulness. In fact, most people know bright college graduates who struggle to resolve everyday problems. Being resourceful takes more than cognitive skill. It takes the ability to process information emotionally as well as intellectually. Research shows that resourceful young people are not only better at achieving their goals, but also respond better under stress. In fact, one study showed that academic stress adversely impacted the grades of students who were low in resourcefulness, but had no impact on the grades of highly resourceful students (Akgun & Ciarrochi, 2003).

In recent years, we've come to recognize the set of brain processes that help children achieve their goals as executive functioning skills. Housed in the frontal lobes, they help children plan, start, oversee, and finish tasks—big and small. It is these same skills that enable young people to chart fulfilling courses through life. When these abilities are weak, everyday living can feel like being on a ship without a rudder. Strong abilities help children see beyond everyday solutions, not giving up when problems get complicated, and learning from mistakes along the way.

Executive functioning skills play a primary role in how children learn to self-regulate and direct their day-to-day and long-term actions. But it is also important to teach the broader concept of how to become a resourceful person and why this matters in life. Children learn resourcefulness through the practice of being goal-directed.

Victor's Story

Parents, teachers, and mentors provide environments that foster resourcefulness when they encourage young people to plan, strategize, prioritize, set goals, seek resources, and monitor their progress. When adults challenge young people to set high expectations and then support youth as they seek to accomplish their goals, they teach them to be flexible and strategic. Youth become adaptable problem-solvers and learn to live without rigid rules or preconceived ideas—essential skills in an increasingly complex world.

When Victor was a sophomore in high school, he reluctantly joined Key Club, a service organization sponsored by Kiwanis International. "I almost didn't get involved," he said, "because I didn't want to follow in my sister's footsteps. But I ended up saying to myself, 'I can join and not be the exact same person as her.'" Victor was encouraged to set goals—and he did. "I decided I wanted to organize a big inter-school soccer tournament that would raise thousands of dollars."

Supported by his parents and the Key Club advisor, Mr. Wolmer, Victor went about planning the tournament. But he didn't achieve the fundraising goals for which he had hoped. Despite his failure, Victor seemed pleased with his learning. "My parents and Mr. Wolmer let me know it was alright. They let me try to plan the event myself—and that was nice for me to get the chance to go out and try to figure out what had to get done." When Victor had questions, he knew he could go to these adults for advice. But he admitted, "No one came to me and said 'I don't think you're planning this the right way,' or 'I don't think you can pull this off.' So it never occurred to me that I couldn't do it—which I think is a big thing."

As Victor reflected on his first experience of trying to achieve a goal in a public way, he said, "It's easy to shy away from doing these things because you think you can't. But once you get over the hump of getting started, things become much easier, especially when you have adult encouragement." From an initial failure, Victor said, "Now I know that the worst thing that can happen is not even trying in the first place."

Victor went on to become the president of Key Club International as a senior in high school and said he learned a lot more about setting goals, strategizing, and planning from "sitting down when I needed help and talking face-to-face with adults who were experienced in getting things done." In college, Victor became a leader with Circle K, the college branch of Kiwanis, as well as the March of Dimes and Building Tomorrow.

CREATIVITY: THE EPICENTER OF EXPLORATION AND DISCOVERY

How do children learn to challenge ideas and think beyond the status quo? How do they develop the attitudes of mind by which to fulfill themselves? Through *creativity*, humans generate and communicate original ideas of value and learn to appreciate the nature of beauty. This process fosters imagination, innovation, and a sense of aesthetics.

In the past decade, a new science of creativity has emerged. Neuroscientists are turning previously-held notions of creativity on their heads, including the fact that creativity does not involve just a single side of the brain. Most scientists agree that creativity must be defined by more than the sum of its parts, which include but are not limited to originality, self-expression, risk-taking, intelligence, autonomy, collaboration, and imagination.

We depend on our creative abilities to help us adapt and thrive in progressively complex and uncertain times. Researchers also believe that a creative life fosters happiness and wellbeing, and that there is a significant connection between creativity, meaning, and intrinsic motivation (Nakamura & Csikszenthihalyi, 2015). Creativity is at the epicenter of human exploration and discovery. Inspired by our senses of sight, sound, taste, touch, and smell, creativity is a force that nurtures human development, innovation, and an aesthetic appreciation of the world around us.

Many people associate creativity with those who are gifted and talented. Few would argue that Steve Job's creativity helped produce the iPhone and other innovative Apple products. But creativity is not confined to people of extraordinary intellect or talent—or to big inventions. *Everyone* has creative capacities that evoke originality, like producing a new recipe, conveying a powerful idea through self-expression, or discovering a better way to achieve a desired outcome.

We are beginning to learn new and surprising ways creativity is fostered during childhood and adolescence. Csikszentmihalyi (2014) suggests that talent may be of less importance than encouragement. He cites a wealth of research showing that when adults devote time and energy to children's overall development, they also help young people develop creative talents. It is more important, therefore, to teach children the thought processes and attitudes of mind associated with creativity, like tolerance for ambiguity and openness to experience, than to teach them how to achieve a creative result as perceived by someone else. Creativity must explore intrinsically meaningful ideas as perceived by young people themselves.

Scott's Story

Children are inspired to be creative when adults encourage young people to express themselves and their ideas through writing, poetry, acting, photography, service, art, digital media, business, etc. When adults take notice and praise youth for generating ideas and taking risks, the imaginations of young people blossom.

I interviewed Scott when he was a 21-year-old college student embarking on a new, exciting journey. He had just been awarded $100,000 to fund his own national service campaign aimed at reducing tobacco use in children. He lived and breathed the mission of his organization and was clearly the creative genius behind the scenes as he and his team of volunteers engaged kids from all around the country.

I first mentioned Scott in Chapter 1 as an example of how mentoring combined with meaningful volunteer service is an essential part of how American youth learn to care about others and the world around them. I was curious to understand what motivated and inspired Scott, and how mentors had played a role in shaping his life.

Describing himself as a "very shy, very quiet" ninth grader, Scott spoke openly about the kind of program and mentor that catapulted an African American kid from North Carolina's tobacco country to create and lead his own social movement. Scott was first attracted to working with a small anti-tobacco campaign in North Carolina because it wasn't the typical kind of menial work where adults tell you what to do. "The fact that it was youth to youth was a huge draw," he said. "They made it seem like you didn't have to be perfect, that they would help you. I thought that was cool—they met me at my own level."

When Scott spoke of Bonnie, the mentor in the local program, he said, "She let youth play a huge role. She gave us guidance, but left the control to us. That's what works when you're trying to motivate youth. You've got to make them feel like they've got some type of role and some importance. That's what Bonnie did."

Through the kind of mentoring Bonnie provided, and an environment that encouraged kids to express themselves, Scott flourished. He now speaks to young people throughout the U.S. about how to create anti-tobacco programs that work—run by youth, of course.

EMPATHY: THE ROOT OF CARING AND ENGAGED CITIZENSHIP

How do children learn to care enough about others that they reap the personal rewards associated with giving? How do they learn to recognize, feel, and respond to the needs and suffering of other people? When young people develop *empathy*, they not only thrive in school and life, but they also impact their communities in positive, often extraordinary ways.

We have come full circle on *The Compass Advantage*™ framework of eight abilities that teach children how to become the pilots of their own lives. Empathy is situated at "true north" on the compass because it is the driver of caring and compassionate actions in the world. The relationship of empathy to self-awareness, at "true south," is symbolic. As it turns out, science suggests that the more aware we become of ourselves, the better we become at knowing and caring for others. By developing empathy in children, we not only help kids feel valued and understood, we impact social change and innovation for decades to come.

Individual and societal success depends on raising and educating children who care about others. But we have misled today's children to believe success is achieved through test scores, material wealth, and personal gain. In turn, there has been a measurable shift toward self-centeredness at a time when society depends more, not less, on people who give of themselves and actively participate in their communities.

While the digital age has given children more ways to connect with others than ever before, many researchers are concerned with how social networking and decreased face-to-face relationships may have contributed toward a 48% drop in empathetic concern for others over the past few decades (Konrath et al., 2011). Not surprisingly, studies have also linked low empathy to increased bullying, narcissism, rigid belief systems, and civic apathy.

Empathy facilitates the expression of caring, compassion, and kindness. The young people who shared their stories with me were average, seemingly normal American kids who managed to develop high levels of empathy and compassion despite Digital Age challenges. Simply stated, they were motivated through empathy-based relationships with people different from themselves. In turn, they were inspired to work toward the betterment of society.

Developed through emotional attachment with other human beings, empathy is extraordinarily complex. It has neurobiological underpinnings in the brain cortex, sub-cortical pathways, autonomic nervous system, hypothalamic-pituitary-adrenal axis, and endocrine systems which work collectively to regulate our emotions, bodily states, and reactivity (Carter et al., 2009). Like other abilities on the compass, it is when children experience empathy systemically with other abilities that each strength becomes greater than itself—a powerful internal pathfinder that contributes to a life of success and wellbeing.

As parents, schools, and communities, we have a moral imperative to rethink how we teach kids to care in a more hurried, impersonal, and data-driven world. By cultivating young people's curiosity about people who are different from themselves, challenging prejudices, and instilling positive values, we help youth expand their capacity to care.

Amar's Story

Adults influence young people's abilities to care for others beyond themselves by creating meaningful relationships with them—by ensuring youth are seen, felt, and understood. When mentors expose young people to different worldviews and encourage them to do meaningful community service, youth develop higher levels of empathy and compassion.

Amar, a 21-year-old college history major, shared a particularly poignant story that illustrates how community service is deeply meaningful when young people develop relationships with people different from themselves. Amar and his Panamanian Hindu parents immigrated to the U.S. when Amar was a young child. Looking back on his high school years, Amar admitted he participated in a few civic activities, "the things every high school student does to get into college."

As a freshman in college, Amar joined a student-initiated service group that was traveling to New Orleans to help rebuild houses after Hurricane Katrina. For him, the idea of building houses was "safe, fun, and an interesting way to get to know other students." Amar confessed that "the physical work was very challenging," but he was able to deal with it because of group camaraderie. But one day, the work took an unexpected turn to the emotional.

The group leader announced that Amar and others would be going into the community to meet families in an effort to find out what additional help they needed. Amar was aghast by this news, saying, "When I first heard we were going door-to-door, I thought it was the most awkward situation that I'd ever heard of in my life. I come from a privileged background. And now you are going to send me around a devastated neighborhood in New Orleans to ask people about their stories? I expected people to slam their doors!"

As Amar reflected on what happened, he said, "It was amazing. People *wanted* to talk to us. In those moments, there were no barriers between us because of race or class, or the fact that we were students." In fact, as Amar pushed his own emotional barriers to connect with families on deeper, empathetic levels, he said, "I realized they were just like my family."

After walking from door-to-door to meet local families, group leaders encouraged students to reflect and talk about the connections and friendships made. Powerful stories were shared. When Amar left New Orleans, there were tears of gratefulness on both sides. The power of empathy would change many lives, including Amar's. He returned to his university and committed himself to issues of homelessness. He went on to become the leader of a project that would make a ten-year commitment to rebuilding homes in New Orleans and returned to those same neighborhoods each year with new groups of students.

CREATING THE CONDITIONS
FOR CHILDREN TO THRIVE

The young people who shared their stories with me did not become civic change makers overnight, or by chance. Like children with other unique interests and goals in life, they learned to flourish from the encouragement of wise, committed adults. When we view healthy youth development as an integrated process of nurturing core abilities, it is easy to see that it is the collaborative efforts of parents, schools, and communities that set up kids for lives of success and well-being. When adults tend to these abilities from early childhood onward, adolescents emerge as caring and compassionate young adults, ready to chart their own meaningful paths through life.

One story that powerfully depicts the transformative power of nurturing the core abilities in *The Compass Advantage*™ was described to me by Jennifer, a young woman with insights beyond her age. Reinforced by years of support and encouragement from a loving family, great teachers, and wise mentors, Jennifer set off to participate in a service-learning project in Cambodia when she was in 10th grade. Jennifer's school had raised enough money to start an elementary school in Cambodia and this was the second year American students visited the campus to work with young Cambodian students.

One day, a few children grabbed Jennifer by the hand, pulled her into a classroom, and wanted her to lead them in doing the Hokey Pokey. At first, Jennifer felt out of her comfort zone. "But I started dancing with them and singing," Jennifer said, "and it was just me and maybe 10 Cambodian students in an empty classroom. The joy that they got out of doing the Hokey Pokey with me was phenomenal."

In the midst of the dancing and singing, Jennifer began to see the world differently. "As we were dancing, putting 'our whole selves in and shaking all about,' I looked down and noticed that a lot of children weren't wearing shoes, and many of them had missing or decaying teeth," Jennifer recalled with a deep sense of empathy. At that moment, Jennifer realized that the words of the song were a metaphor for her experience.

"At the end of every verse," Jennifer said, "I was singing the words 'you do the Hokey Pokey and you turn yourself around, that's what it's all about." She suddenly realized that the time she spent with these young Cambodian children had turned her own life around. "I would never be the same again," Jennifer admitted. "It was that one experience from which I can trace to the interests I have today—not just academic interests or an interest in ending human sex trafficking—but to the belief that I can actually accomplish something in the world. And I will."

These turning points for teenagers, often called critical learning experiences, force young people to confront their values, find meaning, and adopt new perspectives. They rarely happen to young people who have not developed a compass of abilities from which they derive internal guidance. For Jennifer, her experience with Cambodian children caused her to reflect on her privileged life, find purpose, and understand how education is systemically connected to solving social issues.

Before Jennifer graduated from high school, she would speak about her experience in Cambodia at the United Nations. Today, after graduating from Amherst College and working for a nonprofit leader in the fight to eradicate human trafficking, Jennifer is a freshman at Columbia Law School. She chose Columbia from other top schools because of its focus on and commitment to social justice.

Not only are Jennifer and the other young people in this book global change makers, they also represent what all parents and teachers hope for children—to become caring, curious, sociable, resilient, self-aware, honest, resourceful, and creative young adults capable of finding their own ways toward meaningful, fulfilling lives.

Teaching, Parenting, and Mentoring Youth

No one is born a good citizen; no nation is born a democracy. Rather, both are processes that continue to evolve over a lifetime. Young people must be included from birth. A society that cuts off from its youth severs its lifeline.

— Kofi Annan, 7th UN Secretary-General
2001 Nobel Peace Prize Winner

The primary aim of this book is to help bridge the gap between our understanding of civic learning and civic action by better understanding the challenges young people face in community engagement activities. Since Damon (2008) found political and societal interests to be one of the lowest ranking sources of purpose among today's teens, it is important to understand how this relatively small population of young people realized such purposeful pursuits.

For the American youth who participated in my research, civic interests and service beyond self were unusually high sources of motivation. Understanding how these young people coped with challenges and gained perspective and initiative can help develop learning experiences and support systems that foster civic engagement in greater numbers of youth.

Every research study fits into a much bigger body of knowledge. For this reason, Chapter 2 provided a broad perspective of the research that informed my work with civically engaged youth. What happens, though, as a study evolves, additional research contributes to the ongoing conversation, adding value and richness.

I like to compare this process to an imaginary dinner table conversation that begins in a corner of a restaurant. The dialog starts at a small table of diners, but by the time dessert is consumed, the conversation is so compelling that the whole restaurant has chimed in. In this case, we've been listening carefully to stories told by today's youth—stories that provided insights into how they learned from others, found meaning through service, and acted to confront the challenges of civic engagement in ways that fostered their continued initiative. It is through individual and collective initiative that social change and innovation are possible.

What did we learn from their stories? Who else is talking about these insights? What do these stories mean for how we teach, parent, and mentor children on their pathways toward active citizenship? This chapter distills the main insights from my conversations with youth and discusses them in light of the research and their implications for practice.

Through studying the brain, neuroscientists have helped explain why storytelling is so important and how a well-told story contains the kinds of emotions, thoughts, conflicts, and resolutions necessary to gain valuable learning. Developing a civic identity is an ever-changing, constantly unfolding process created by personal, social, and cultural stories. How do we help young people construct life stories that engage them in civic discourse, turn empathy into action, and create innovative social change? From many hours of listening to youth and years of synthesizing relevant research, the following three main findings emerged from this study:

1. Overcoming obstacles increases civic initiative.
2. Adults scaffold engaged citizenship.
3. Transformative learning connects meaning to action.

In the three sections that follow, I expand the conversation about these insights by introducing relevant additional research, as well as how that research is applied in the practice of educating, parenting, and mentoring youth.

OVERCOMING OBSTACLES INCREASES CIVIC INITIATIVE

Erikson (1950) argued that the development of initiative involved overcoming obstacles. My study not only supports that claim, but also suggests a strong relationship between Larson's (2000) research on initiative and Damon's (2008) research on youth purpose. Chapter 2 examined these two bodies of research, particularly how children thrive and develop competencies through mastery experiences that included challenges and obstacles.

The young people's stories in this study supported Larson's (2000) assertion that initiative involves a deep and voluntary investment in an activity, and is experienced in real world environments with ongoing challenges. Students also demonstrated the purposeful civic action that Damon (2008) described as "a stable and generalized intention to accomplish something that is at once meaningful to the self and of consequence to the world beyond the self" (p. 33).

Beyond Traditional Classrooms

This study showed that the development of civic initiative and purpose are highly influenced by young people's abilities to overcome challenges in community service and service-learning experiences. It validated the work of other researchers who drew similar conclusions about the importance of overcoming challenges and obstacles in the real world—outside traditional classrooms—to positive youth development (Bandura, 1994, 2001; Damon, 2008; Erikson, 1950; Jennings & Niemi, 1981; Kahne & Sporte, 2008; Larson, 2000; Larson & Walker, 2005).

My research outlines distinctions in the types of challenges found in civic activities and the differing roles played by intellectual, interpersonal, and intrapersonal challenges. Students related overcoming intellectual challenges to gains in critical thinking, planning, organizing, and problem solving. This supports Larson and Hansen's (2005) findings that a deeper understanding of differing perspectives and human systems emerges as a result of overcoming civic challenges. Gains in development were also linked to challenges in both studies. However, Larson and Hansen did not distinguish types of challenges in their research.

Challenges Become Motivators

Breaking new ground, my research revealed a deeper understanding of the emotional challenges of civic engagement, a dimension not examined by Larson and Hansen (2005). Although Larson (2000) defined initiative as "the ability to be motivated from within to direct attention and effort toward a challenging goal" (p. 170), the inner aspect of motivation is largely ignored in the civic engagement research.

The young people in this study reported emotional, out-of-comfort-zone challenges as their number one source of motivation and purpose. In fact, all of the young people pointed to specific intrapersonal challenges that transformed their understanding of civic engagement and motivated them from within to adopt social or environmental causes. These challenges always invited internal moral-ethical reasoning that produced new meaning and changes of perspective.

Moral Dilemmas Help Define Identity

Erikson (1950) first discussed initiative within the context of morality and moral responsibility. Kohlberg (1981, 1984) posited that moral reasoning, the basis for ethical behavior, helped children and adults respond to moral dilemmas. In this study, the intrapersonal challenges of civic engagement were related to the struggle with moral dilemmas, supporting Erikson's and Kohlberg's thinking, and validating the work of other researchers who have linked moral development with civic commitment, self-concept, and identity (Colby & Damon, 1992; Hart & Fegley, 1995; Youniss & Yates, 1999).

My research further suggests that the ability to identify and reflect on moral issues during and following emotionally intense service experiences may facilitate the development of civic identity. Situations that take young people to the edge of their emotional comfort zones likely ignite internal moral struggles that, in turn, help define identity and purpose. Recent studies that show strong relationships between purpose, moral development, and civic engagement support this thinking (Damon, 2008; Damon et al., 2003; Schneider & Stevenson, 1999).

Initiative and Purpose are Interconnected

This study suggests that the cognitive and emotional aspects of development in these young citizens are systemically related. Dewey (1938) first posited that the cognitive element of initiative was related to purpose when he said, "The formation of purposes and the organization of means to execute them are the work of intelligence" (p. 62).

The highly purposeful youth in this study would not likely have had transformative intrapersonal civic experiences without the cognitive abilities gained from facing intellectual and interpersonal challenges along the way. In fact, these cognitive gains were reported by all students. Improved abilities to critically think, plan, analyze, problem-solve, and interact with others likely gave young people the means to execute their chosen purposes, creating paths from civic learning to civic action.

Larson (2000) posited that initiative development required three elements that must be experienced together: (a) a deep desire to be involved, (b) experience in an environment that contains challenges and complexities of the real world, and (c) events that transpire over a period of time. While my study corroborated the importance of these three elements, it does not appear that these elements are always experienced together.

For example, youth may benefit from the intellectual and interpersonal challenges of civic engagement even when they do not feel deeply invested in activities. In fact, the advantages they gain from those challenges may, as Dewey (1938) suggested, provide the intellectual capacity to process deeper intrapersonal challenges that involve moral dilemmas. It may explain why one young man had a transformative experience when he encountered homelessness in New Orleans while his classmate gawked and took photos to show his friends back home.

Like other participants in this study, the first young man had the intellectual capacity gained from other life experiences. His encounter with homelessness also evoked deep moral discernment from which he constructed new meaning. This single intrapersonal challenge changed his perspective and ignited a deep desire to be involved with homelessness. Damon (2008) named this deep desire purpose. Every student in this study linked a transformative intrapersonal challenge to a change in perspective, a change that could not have occurred without critical thinking skills.

Section Summary

The first main finding—that overcoming obstacles increases civic initiative—suggests that the challenges of civic involvement engaged both cognition and emotion, facilitating the development of youth purpose and initiative in this study's population. These challenges also compelled young people to morally discern right from wrong. Purpose, what Damon (2008) described as a source of motivation, may be synonymous with what Larson (2000) described as the "ability to be motivated from within" (p. 170).

Young people clearly articulated civic purposes that were fostered by learning at the edge, by facing emotional challenges that pushed their boundaries of understanding. These challenges always included internal moral discourse. Civic purposes were executed by the "work of intelligence" (Dewey, 1938, p. 62) as participants engaged in efforts to accomplish challenging goals. A dynamic relationship between purpose, initiative, and moral reasoning existed in this study's highly engaged population.

ADULTS SCAFFOLD ENGAGED CITIZENSHIP

The concept of scaffolding was first used to describe the process of supporting a young child "to solve a problem, carry out a task or achieve a goal which would be beyond his unassisted efforts" (Wood, Bruner, & Ross, 1976, p. 90). It was expanded by others, including Vygotsky (1978), to describe the interactional support by which adults fostered children's efforts to learn. While it is most often used in the context of teaching cognitive skills like math and language, this study suggests that adult mentors, parents, and program leaders also scaffold the development of moral development and critical thinking as well as internal strengths like self-efficacy. In turn, these attributes bolster a young person's capacity to successfully engage in civil society.

Pea (2004) offered more evidence for relational scaffolding and linked it to social practices that have occurred in parenting and other forms of caring over millennia. Rather than taking charge, young people described helpful adults as being in the background—mentoring, facilitating, and monitoring. When young people gained self-confidence and skills, adult participation faded. They moved forward, providing feedback, friendship, and more limited direct support. Such fading, according to Pea, "is an intrinsic component of the scaffolding framework" (p. 431).

Research studies in political socialization have long shown correlation between exposure to civic role models and higher levels of civic engagement (Jennings & Niemi, 1981; Kahne & Sporte, 2008; Sears, 1975; Zukin et al., 2006). While this study found civic role models played an inspirational role in motivation, it did not find evidence they provided developmental scaffolding.

Non-Parent Mentors Nurture Self-Efficacy

This study uncovered a clear distinction between civic role models and non-parent adult mentors. Young people's stories supplied consistent evidence that one-to-one relationships with adult mentors, most often high school educators, afforded the scaffolding that helped them develop a belief in themselves. And they attributed that belief to the people they had become.

While civic role models sometimes doubled as adult mentors, most participants reported that adult mentors did not focus on either their academic or civic activities. Rather, mentors were singularly committed to their growth as individuals. Bandura (1994, 2001) believed that positive social role models were essential to acquiring self-efficacy. This study not only validates that belief, but also supports the work of Larson (2000) who makes a strong connection between self-efficacy, initiative, and civic engagement.

This study suggests that mentors provided the scaffolding for the development of self-efficacy by supporting and encouraging, listening, setting high personal expectations, showing interest in youth as individuals, fostering self-decision making, and providing another perspective during problem-solving. The importance of adult mentors has been linked to positive youth development in other studies (Benson, 1997; Fergus & Zimmerman, 2005). Students considered these mentors friends and most often stayed in touch with them as college students.

While adult mentors were most often teachers and school administrators, their one-on-one mentoring took place outside the classroom, supporting Bandura's (2001) contention that traditional classrooms were not environments conducive to developing self-efficacy. The ways in which young people described their adult mentors is reminiscent of the way Greenleaf (1977) described servant-leaders. Those mentored by servant-leaders, according to Greenleaf, grow as individuals, become more autonomous and wise, and are more likely to become servant-leaders themselves. This thinking led to the development of *The Compass Advantage*™ framework outlined in Chapter 6, designed to help parents, schools, and communities understand the core principles that help young people thrive in life.

Families Instill Moral Values

Moral development has been related to civic engagement and collective civic agency by numerous researchers (Colby & Damon, 1992; Damon, 2003, 2008; Hart & Fegley, 1995; Schneider & Stevenson, 1999; Yates & Youniss, 1996; Youniss & Yates, 1997). While many programs and religious institutions played a key role in scaffolding character development, this research found civically engaged youth mostly attributed moral values to their families of origin. Even when adolescents rejected the values, religion, or political views of parents, they acknowledged the impact of those views on the citizens they became.

Parents instilled positive values by exemplifying how to live in moral ways. They also encouraged and supported their children's interests and showed them how to overcome obstacles. Rather than controlling how children thought, parents encouraged children to think for themselves. This finding illustrated the type of informational environment described by Deci and Ryan (1985) who also posited that it nurtured intrinsic motivation. In contrast, Kahne and Sporte (2008) found that controlling home environments were negatively correlated with civic engagement.

Again, the role and timing of scaffolding seemed important. As parents engaged children's learning through moral example and guidance with problem-solving, scaffolding as described by Pea (2004) was faded during adolescence to allow children more freedom to overcome their own challenges and obstacles. Civic engagement provided a rich context in which to experience these challenges. For research participants, this freedom most likely facilitated their transformative civic experiences, allowing them to struggle with moral issues and discover their own purposes.

Youth Program Leaders Foster Internal Abilities

Like other researchers, the findings of my study show how youth gain critical thinking and problem-solving skills through challenging civic engagement programs that provided real-world experiences (Larson, 2000; Larson & Hansen, 2005; Larson et al., 2005). Findings also suggest, as have other researchers, that the supportive relationships, encouragement, and skill-building opportunities provided by program leaders were highly valuable (Eccles & Gootman, 2002; Yohalem & Wilson-Ahlstrom, 2007).

Finally, this research demonstrated that young people learn—and have transformative experiences—even in programs where leaders do not always respond in desired ways. In fact, many of the challenges and obstacles of civic engagement were related to program leadership and structure.

Regardless of program structures or leadership styles, study participants reported enormous personal growth and development as a product of their participation. Youniss, McLellan, and Yates (1997) showed the developmental benefits of organized programs across many types, including civic, business, political, and religious.

While adult mentors and parents provided and faded scaffolding in the more traditional understanding of the concept, young people built their own scaffolding when it came to programs. They chose programs based on their own interests. When they felt unchallenged, they asked for greater responsibility. When one program did not meet their needs, they found different opportunities. Scaffolding naturally faded when it was no longer needed.

This self-directed process related to program choice evoked Erikson's (1950) thinking that adolescents chose activities that cultivate important competencies and social networks. Bandura (1994) also argued that if adolescents are insulated from making their own choices during this period, they do not learn to navigate through problems, a necessary ingredient of initiative and self-efficacy.

This study's findings validate this thinking and further suggest that inner strengths, like purpose, initiative, moral reasoning, self-efficacy, and critical thinking are foundational to the development of highly engaged citizens. Diener (2009) corroborates this assessment, proposing that the traditional assumptions about community service and service-learning must be challenged to consider ways in which inner strengths are developed.

Section Summary

The second main finding—that adults scaffold engaged citizenship—suggests that adult support is essential to developing the internal strengths of young people who become highly engaged in civic causes. Long-term adult mentors and parents played a significant role in scaffolding self-efficacy and moral development. Similar to Greenleaf's (1977) servant leadership theory, high school educators and other non-parent adult mentors helped adolescents grow as individuals through one-on-one supportive mentoring relationships. Families of origin instilled moral values, scaffolded problem-solving and encouraged children to think for themselves in the kinds of informational environments depicted by Deci and Ryan (1985).

Bolstered by supportive mentors and parents, adolescents self-directed and scaffolded their own community service choices, weighed opportunities, and faced obstacles—important developmental processes described by Erikson (1950) and Bandura (1994). These programs and their leaders provided opportunities to develop critical thinking and problem-solving skills in the real world. Pea's (2004) relational scaffolding framework helped to understand how the combined efforts of families, schools, and communities supported the positive development of highly engaged youth.

TRANSFORMATIVE LEARNING CONNECTS
MEANING TO ACTION

Erikson (1968) believed that young people need to find meaning as they established their identities within the societal framework. Along with the work of Damon et al. (2003) and Youniss (2006), the findings of this study suggest that the construction of meaning is highly associated with the development of purpose, initiative, and civic identity. The study identified self-reflectiveness as a key ability in the meaning construction process among participants. Self-reflectiveness has been consistently correlated with civic engagement in young people (Andolina et al., 2003; Colby & Sullivan, 2009, Winter; Kahne & Sporte, 2008; Wuthnow, 1995; Youniss & Yates, 1997, 1999; Zukin et al., 2006).

Service is Rich Context for Learning

The findings of this study expand previous studies through exploration of how meaning is constructed from the intrapersonal challenges of civic engagement and suggest these challenges are rich contexts for transformative learning. This type of learning is not typically referenced in the youth developmental or civic engagement literatures. It is probably best understood through Mezirow's (1991) transformative learning theory situated in the research on adult development. The elements required for transformative learning include a disorienting dilemma that serves as a catalyst for change and critical reflection. The outcome of transformative learning is perspective change. Learning that is transformative in nature has been correlated with the development of purpose and life mission in adulthood (Kovan & Dirkx, 2003; Kroth & Boverie, 2000). It often involves a deep shift in how people see themselves, their relationships with others and the world, and approaches to peace and social justice (Morrell & O'Connor, 2002).

Commitment Evolves from Purpose and Meaning

The stories of highly committed youth suggest their sustained civic engagement arose from a deep sense of purpose and meaning. This finding echoes the findings of researchers who retrospectively explored the lives of adult activists (Colby & Damon, 1992; Teske, 1997b). The young people in this study reported episodes of deep learning following specific disorienting moral dilemmas associated with community service. These dilemmas most often occurred when participants came face-to-face with less privileged populations or other situations that involved human suffering.

The young adults in this study dealt with these disorienting dilemmas by turning inward to discover more about themselves and their worlds through self-reflection. Scaffolded by adult mentors, they found encouragement, support, and acceptance through non-parent relationships that allowed them to openly share thoughts and feelings. The qualities of these relationships correlated with many relational attributes in the literature on adult transformative learning (Taylor, 2007).

Ideology is Shaped During Adolescence

Transformative stories always ended with perspective change, a shift associated with a deeper understanding of education, social change, privilege, or human relationships. Like their adult counterparts in Kroth and Boverie's (2000) research, these life-changing experiences led 73% of young adults in this study to develop career-life purposes related to their civic activities. The relationship between transformative learning and action is widely acknowledged by researchers (Berger, 2004; Taylor, 2007).

Erikson (1950) observed that adolescence is a time when youth confront ideology and values, and develop a sense of morality that remains a lifetime. He later made repeated use of the term ideology, proposing that it provided a way of making meaning from life experiences (Erikson, 1968). The participants in this study illustrated this process, particularly as they faced challenges that pushed them out of their emotional comfort zones. It was during and following these challenges that they confronted the values and moral upbringings from their families of origin to make meaning from critical experiences.

Moral Dilemmas Help Form Civic Identity

The young people in this study confronted issues that were both morally relevant and self-regarding at the same time, a process that created internal struggle. For example, almost all students talked about the conflict they felt between helping others and what they personally gained as a result of their service. This is reminiscent of Teske's (1997b) research with adult activists that found moral motivation in political behavior was not rooted solely in self-interest or solely on altruistic impulses, but the struggle between them was part of the identity-construction process.

This study suggests that the traditional sources of ideology, particularly religion and political beliefs, may be changing for today's youth. While the highly engaged population in this study approached their civic commitments with religious zeal, most did not consider themselves religious. In fact, 40% self-identified as atheist or agnostic and less than one percent said they were deeply motivated by faith in God. This is quite different from the adult moral exemplars interviewed by Colby and Damon (1992) who were motivated by strong commitments to faith. Several recent articles may inform this surprising finding, suggesting that today's youth are not as connected to faith as were previous generations (Gonzales, 2007; Goodstein, 2006).

Caring is Central to Justice-Oriented Leadership

More than half of study participants identified themselves as politically independent yet they were as likely to be as politically engaged as those who identified with a political party. Similar to findings on religious affiliations, this represents a change from what we know about older generations. Adults who consider themselves independent are less likely to vote or participate in activities that influence government action than their party-affiliated counterparts (Hetheringon, 2008).

Regardless of religious or political backgrounds, what seemed to be a driving ideology for most participants was a belief in a caring, just, and sustainable society. Some researchers have commented on this ideological shift, predicting that globalism and technological advances of the information age have made this generation of youth more acutely aware of social justice issues around the world and given them additional tools to tackle global problems (Howe & Strauss, 2000; Zukin et al., 2006).

Westheimer and Kahne (2004) pointed to the need to develop young citizens with an ideological propensity toward social justice and collective social action. In fact, being identified as a participatory or justice-oriented citizen as defined by Westheimer and Kahne was one criterion used to select interviewees for this study. All participants met Westheimer and Kahne's definition of a personally responsible citizen, and had related character traits such as self-discipline, integrity, honesty, compassion, and high morals. In fact, they listed many of these attributes as strengths they developed as a result of community service, family, or religious upbringings.

Citizenship is Interest Dependent

Although Westheimer and Kahne (2004) defined three distinct citizen types, the traits of the personally responsible citizen seemed to provide a foundation for the making of the participatory and justice-oriented citizens in this study. Findings also suggest that whether participants acted responsibly, took leadership roles in civic programs, or explored the root causes of social problems was directly related to the meaning they constructed from their civic experiences and the purposeful causes they adopted.

For example, some young people who would be considered justice-oriented on issues related to world hunger might become more participatory or responsible on issues related to the environment. Having acquired critical thinking and problem-solving skills, they seemed poised to become situational citizens, those who could respond through the lens of any of the three citizen types, depending on their interests. Differences in their motivation from one situation to another seemed to stem from a combination of meaning-making and self-defined civic purposes. Over time, this process of meaning-making helped them form civic identities.

Civic Identity Unfolds Over Time

While young people in this study formed engaged civic identities through diverse service experiences, they described the process of identity construction as an unfolding journey of learning, meaning-making, skill development, and personal awareness that occurred over time. Participant stories supported Erikson's (1950) observations that teens drew on prior strengths to face subsequent challenges and that they confronted ideology and values as part of the identity development process.

Providing a helpful framework for this study, Erikson emphasized the inner aspects of identity as well as the social aspects that helped youth form a relationship with society. The findings of this study support the conclusions of Yates and Youniss (1996) who argued that civic identity is associated with agency, social relatedness, and moral–political awareness. It also validates their thesis that service activities which provide opportunities for intense experiences and social interactions are linked to prosocial development.

Based on recurrent themes from participants' stories, four characteristics appear to characterize civic identity formation: (a) development over time through the dynamic interplay between service opportunities, morality, and adult scaffolding; (b) the ability to face and gain from intellectual, interpersonal, and intrapersonal challenges; (c) reflection and meaning-making based on multiple experiences; and (d) integration of one's activities into a meaningful way of life rather than a collection of service experiences.

Section Summary

The third main finding—that transformative learning connects meaning to action—implies that challenging service experiences during adolescence helps bolster long-term civic identity. Community service and service-learning opportunities were rich contexts for learning that closely mirrored Mezirow's (1991) adult transformative learning theory.

Intense challenges and obstacles that pushed young people to the edge of their intellectual and emotional boundaries were catalysts for self-reflection and meaning-making for youth in this study. Civic learning that included out-of-comfort-zone experiences resulted in perspective changes that caused young people to shift the way they saw their roles as global citizens and their approaches to social and environmental justice. Over time, young people developed engaged civic identities that became a way of life.

NEW CONTRIBUTIONS TO RESEARCH

This study drew from multidisciplinary research to learn from the stories of young people who sustained high levels of civic engagement during adolescence and into their college years. While findings supported the research of many others who have studied civic engagement and positive youth development, this study broke new ground in three important ways.

First, the use of narrative methodology to study how young people described and learned from the challenges and obstacles of civic engagement produced a systemic understanding of engaged, activist youth not previously found in the literature. This study identified nine characteristics that were essential to participants as they developed into engaged citizens. Initiative, purpose, moral reasoning, moral development, self-efficacy, critical thinking, self-reflection, ideology, and civic identity have been individually studied by numerous researchers (Andolina et al., 2003; Bandura, 2001; Colby & Damon, 1992; Colby & Sullivan, 2009, Winter; Damon, 2003, 2008; Hart & Fegley, 1995; Kahne & Sporte, 2008; Kohlberg, 1981, 1984; Larson, 2000; Larson & Hansen, 2005; Larson et al., 2005; Schneider & Stevenson, 1999; Teske, 1997b; Wuthnow, 1995; Yates & Youniss, 1996; Youniss et al., 1997; Youniss & Yates, 1999; Zukin et al., 2006).

Taken together, this study found a relationship between them that, through further research, may offer a new conceptual understanding of citizenship development and how these attributes are interconnected. Through this systemic lens, it may be easier to recognize how families, schools, and communities influence the development of future citizens.

Second, this study expanded our understanding of the challenges and obstacles of civic engagement, particularly the emotional challenges that involved face-to-face interactions with people who were suffering. These intense emotional encounters provided disorienting moral dilemmas for participants that served as catalysts for critical reflection and perspective change.

While transformative learning has been researched and discussed in adult development, this study suggests that this type of learning can also take place in adolescence, and that emotionally intense civic experiences are rich contexts for transformation. It also suggests that transformative learning during adolescence is critical to developing initiative, purpose, and civic identity in young adults.

Third, how adults scaffold the development of young citizens was a key contribution of this study. Particularly important was the role that high school educators and other non-parent adult mentors played in the development of self-efficacy, an important characteristic of civically engaged youth.

While previous research emphasized the importance of civic role models, the participants in this study clearly differentiated non-parent mentors from traditional notions of civic role models. Young people recognized the major role these mentors played in nurturing a belief in self, without which they would not have become the engaged young adults they are today.

Most scholars agree that numerous precursors to civic engagement exist before the formative adolescent and young adult years. Although this study uncovered some of those precursors during the retrospective interview process, it was limited by its focus on adolescent and young adult experiences, relationships, and contexts. While using exemplars provides insights on highly engaged young people, it does not provide information on disengaged youth and how to change patterns of disengagement and disenfranchisement.

Despite these and other limitations, this study provided an opportunity to deeply explore a particular population of civically engaged young people in multiple contexts, adding to the literature on how young people traverse the path from civic learning to civic action. Much can be learned by studying young people who excel in certain areas. While statements cannot be made that compare them to non-engaged youth, their experiences further our understanding of how to improve programs and support for all young people.

TOPICS FOR FUTURE RESEARCH

Researchers can make useful contributions to understanding how young people are motivated to engage in civil society by studying examples of youth who display high levels of engagement. While this study was limited by sample size and methodology, participants provided valuable insights into the challenges of engagement and how learning accompanied those challenges. This study is one of the first to focus on a highly engaged group of young citizens and it offers a rich lead to future investigation.

Systemic Nature of Citizenship Development

Further research might expand our understanding of the relationship between the nine characteristics of engaged youth identified in this study: initiative, purpose, moral reasoning, moral development, self-efficacy, critical thinking, self-reflection, ideology, and civic identity. While we understand a great deal about these concepts individually, the interconnectedness of one to the others seems particularly important to developing a systemic framework that enhances our abilities to engage youth in civic society. Additional studies are needed to expand our understanding of these related concepts and how they are dynamically nurtured in young people. Such research may develop a new conceptual understanding of citizenship development.

Transformative Learning in Adolescence

Further studies might illuminate the intrapersonal challenges of civic engagement and the potential transformative learning that results from those experiences. While Mezirow's (1991) transformative learning theory is situated in the adult development literature, it offers insights into understanding the profound and life-changing effects that service-learning can have on adolescents. Expanded awareness of this literature might facilitate the development of civic programs, curriculum, and service-learning that push youth to expand the boundaries of their thinking. It is at these edges of learning that transformation is most possible (Berger, 2004).

The study of transformative civic action and learning during adolescence must consider the contexts in which disorienting dilemmas occur. Are they more likely to take place in developing countries that face extreme poverty and hardships? Or are there local opportunities through homeless shelters, nursing homes, or other places where young people face moral dilemmas that shape the citizens they become? If transformative experiences involve face-to-face encounters with people who are less privileged or suffering, how can the least privileged of American youth be afforded opportunities for such learning?

Youth from Disadvantaged Backgrounds

Future research must expand our understanding of how youth from low-income families achieve higher levels of civic participation and leadership. Studies that examine the lived experiences of highly engaged youth from disadvantaged backgrounds would provide valuable insights into understanding pathways to civic engagement for this population. While this study included a diversity of family income levels and suggested common themes between them, a more thorough examination of less privileged American youth would add to the research.

Role of High School Educators

High school educators played a surprising and significant role in the lives of the youth in this study. It would be useful to know how these relationships and other non-parent adult mentors facilitate the development of self-efficacy and other internal strengths young people need to successfully engage in civic society.

Obviously, educators can only form a limited number of close mentoring relationships outside the classroom. Researchers might examine the nature of these relationships from the perspective of both teachers and students. What draws teachers into mentoring relationships with particular students? What challenges do teachers face as mentors? Do the choices that teachers make empower some youth and marginalize others?

Since teachers cannot possibly provide mentoring for all young people, what other community resources can be expanded to better fulfill this role in children's lives? How can non-parent adult mentors be trained to facilitate growth in young people?

Developmental Scaffolding

It would also be helpful to more fully examine the concept of developmental scaffolding. For example, in adult mentoring relationships, how does scaffolding fade as students gain self-efficacy? How does the relationship change as the result of fading? How do mentors and students recognize this change? Research on how parents scaffold moral development, critical thinking, and self-decision making in children would provide helpful guidance to parents on important elements of developing initiative and purpose in young people.

Changing Generational Trends

While we know from national surveys that religious faith and political affiliation are common motivators of young people's civic engagement (Levine, 2007), faith and affiliation were relatively unimportant for the participants in this study. Yet despite the high numbers of non-ideologues and political independents, young people were highly engaged in improving the lives of others and influencing government action.

Research that more deeply examines the ideological propensity of today's highly engaged youth compared to their adult counterparts of previous generations may provide additional answers to the types of service-learning programs that spark social action. Such research might confirm changing trends or generational shifts from more traditional sources of ideology, such as religion, politics, or ethnic affiliations, to broader beliefs in a more caring, just, and sustainable world. Longitudinal studies might track changes in this population as they grow into adulthood.

IMPLICATIONS FOR PRACTICE

Most studies suggest at least several specific recommendations that should be considered in real-world practice. For example, what knowledge was gained from this study that can be directly applied to classroom learning, community service experiences, mentoring, and parenting youth? Cited earlier in this chapter, this study certainly supports others that question the abilities of traditional classrooms to develop initiative, purpose, self-efficacy, and civic-efficacy during adolescence. It calls upon educators and policy makers to rethink how we foster the development of future social and environmental change makers. Furthermore, it connects civic identity development to broader core abilities gained during childhood and adolescence, implying that citizenship development is the shared responsibility of families, schools, and communities. This study also suggests the following implications for practice, summarized in the four sections that follow.

Bring Transformative Learning to Traditional Classrooms

The story provided by Danielle in Chapter 4 that described her geography class is a shining example of one teacher who used a traditional classroom subject to engage students in the real world. His efforts were transformative for hundreds of students, pushed beyond textbook learning to change the way they saw themselves and the world. Curriculum developers can apply the experiences of this teacher and others who have expanded the boundaries of instructional teaching to a process of engagement with learning experiences.

This type of learning, most often defined as andragogy, is historically associated with adult learning theory. One of the most important findings from this research was that high school students develop engaged civic identities through learning methods traditionally found in literature on adult learners. While they are still developing abilities to critically think and analyze information, adolescents are also capable of dealing with disorienting dilemmas, reflecting on moral implications, and achieving perspective change.

Developers of school curriculum, civic programs, and service-learning should be aware of the literature on adulthood that contains ways to foster transformative learning in practice (Taylor, 2007). Service combined with learning contains important pedagogical entry points that help young people make sense of experiences and their systemic implications in the world.

Increase Opportunities for Reflective Thinking

The young people in this study were highly self-reflective. They reflected on moral issues during and following emotionally intense service experiences, and this reflection was an important catalyst for enduring civic engagement. This finding has practical implications, suggesting that opportunities for reflection and open discussion may help some young people more fully experience and understand the implications of service.

Those who lead and structure service-learning programs may help facilitate important inner processes like reflection by allowing time and providing provocative questions that identify feelings and stimulate critical thinking. This implication for practice, however, has caveats. While the young adults in this study were open to self-reflection, all youth are not. Leaders must facilitate reflection in ways that meet young people's individual needs.

Be Servant Leaders to Young People

Adults scaffold young people's civic learning when they recognize, understand, and impact a range of internal abilities in children. These abilities, described in *The Compass Advantage*™ framework introduced in Chapter 6, include curiosity, sociability, resilience, self-awareness, integrity, resourcefulness, creativity, and empathy. Together, these abilities give young people a sense of self-efficacy and the skills to become innovative change makers. Quite frankly, they are abilities that all children need to succeed in school, careers, and life.

Adults nurture children's internal compasses when they *connect* with youth, especially when young people seem confused, or when they attempt to chart new ground. They listen for questions that push teens to the edges of their comfort zones. They support them. In the foreword to Greenleaf's (1977) original treatise on servant leadership, Steven Covey defined a servant leader as "one who seeks to draw out, inspire, and develop the best and highest within people from the inside out" (p. 3).

This image of a servant leader is precisely the role that adult mentors, parents, civic role models, and program leaders played in the lives of young people in this study. The field of positive youth development focuses on the internal strengths of each child (Damon, 2004). Using the vast resources from the fields of servant leadership and youth development would be particularly valuable in refining training programs that teach the art of mentoring adolescents.

Provide Opportunities for All Children

Lastly, it is easy to agree that children from low-income families need the same opportunities as other young people to grow into engaged citizens with voices in democracy. Yet, in practice, this outcome has been difficult to achieve. While this study contained only a handful of youth who grew up with a scarcity of resources, those few provided deep insights for practice.

It was not the act of volunteering that provided teens with opportunities to face and learn from the challenges of civic engagement. Some joined causes that gave them stipends, chances to travel, and skill training. They began doing civic work not from altruistic impulses, but for external reasons, mostly to better themselves. Some needed money to buy small things in life that other kids took for granted. But as luck would have it, they ended up in programs that provided transformative experiences, found encouraging adult mentors, and realized how supportive families and friends helped them grow.

It is imperative that we challenge the traditional ways we view volunteerism, particularly for the most disadvantaged. Can they be lifted to new roles within society by financially supporting civic engagement activities in middle and high school? This study would support consideration of this practice, with careful attention to studying outcomes.

CONCLUDING THOUGHTS

While the problems of civil society are immensely complex and daunting, the young people in this study inspire hope. It is the task of each generation to take up the burdens of renewing society and to make its own history. Some assert that contemporary youth are not equipped to tackle these burdens, pointing to the multitude of bad press on today's more narcissistic young people.

Yet the young adults in this study, and thousands like them, are making a difference through collective efforts to improve society. Their work often goes unnoticed because they are not troubled youth. Neither are they likely to be star athletes. They are simply committed, motivated, and engaged adolescents who care about the planet and collectively act to make it a more caring, just, and sustainable place to live.

What did these young people have in common? After analyzing hundreds of pages of narrative stories, three interrelated words trickled to the bottom of my huge data funnel: *opportunity, morality,* and *scaffolding*.

The engaged youth in this study had opportunity—chances to serve through programs that expanded the boundaries of their thinking and pushed them to the edges of civic learning. They were young people who paid attention to issues of morality—choosing codes of conduct and beliefs that showed respect, empathy, and fairness to others. Lastly, they had the benefits of adult scaffolding—wise helpers who kept them on track, provided resources, set high expectations, fostered self-decision making, and encouraged them to believe in themselves.

Opportunity. Morality. Scaffolding.

Three simple words.

One powerful result.

Acknowledgements

A few words of gratitude seem insufficient for the time, support, and encouragement of so many people.

First and foremost, thanks to the young people who shared their stories, insights, and learning with me. While they were all busy college students with demanding schedules, each took the time to fully contribute to my research. A special thanks to the students who agreed to in-depth interviews, speaking openly and honestly about their civic experiences and challenges. All participants were role models for future generations and offer hope that today's global social and environmental issues are in capable hands.

The young citizens in this book helped me reflect on my own journey to developing a civic identity. What I learned from them helped me acknowledge the following important people in my own life, without whom this book would not have been written. I am grateful to my parents, Dorothy Latimer Dennis and Herman Dennis, for instilling moral values in their children. I am deeply appreciative of Judy Czarnecki Stark, my high school teacher, mentor, and friend, whose support and encouragement helped me believe in myself. I am thankful to my first civic role model, Patsy Chandler, who modeled service beyond self and how to overcome life's challenges. Lastly, I am indebted to the people of Haiti, who in 1969 transformed my perspective of those living in poverty and inspired my life-long commitment to social justice.

I owe a debt of gratitude to a small group of academic mentors at Fielding Graduate University who challenged me to think and learn beyond my wildest imagination. Judy Stevens-Long, PhD, nurtured my study's concept from tiny seeds to flourishing branches of inquiry. In the process, she helped me become a better writer and student of human development. Katrina Rogers, PhD, helped awaken the avid researcher inside me. With every insightful question, she inspired me to follow new leads and possibilities. Keith Melville, PhD, taught me the tenets of good critical thinking. His gentle leadership style and wise advice led me to integrate my interests in youth development and civic engagement. Randy Byrnes, PhD, was a wonderful cheerleader, friend, and razor-sharp editor. His rich sense of humor brought many memorable smiles to this project. Lastly, I am particularly indebted to Peter Levine, PhD, of the Jonathan M. Tisch College of Citizenship and Public Service at Tufts University for taking time out of his busy schedule to oversee this research. Peter's contributions to the field of youth civic engagement are renowned and his insights offered invaluable guidance.

I want to express appreciation to the following friends and colleagues who especially encouraged and supported my work through eight years of doctoral and post-doctoral studies: Cezanne Allan, MD; Ana Barrio, PhD; Jane Cartmell; Faith Chapel; Susan Grijalva; Lynda Hamilton; Paula J. Hillmann, PhD; Trudi Inslee; Brenda Kaulback, PhD; Jeff Leinaweaver, PhD; Ellen Lockert, Patti Millar, PhD; Stephen Murphy-Shigematsu, PhD; Sharon Stanley, PhD; Rosemary Talmadge, PhD; Jennifer Waldron, PhD; and Donna Zajonc.

Many people contributed valued talent, support, and guidance as I made my way into the world of blogging, social media, book writing, and publishing. Thank you to my agent, Elizabeth Kaplan, for believing in my work and in the values of positive youth development. Thank you to Lee Kravitz for your time and insights on writing compelling narratives. Thank you to Dan Blank for pushing me to find and build an audience of valued readers at *RootsOfAction.com,* and to Jennie Nash for helping me refine my voice as a writer. Thank you to Lybi Ma, Senior Editor at *Psychology Today,* and to Kristen Franklin, Managing Editor at *Edutopia* and The George Lucas Educational Foundation for giving me the opportunity to share articles about positive youth development with a large international audience. Thanks to Dr. Michele Borba for long phone chats, good laughs, and camaraderie as we struggled with the solo work of writing and researching in our shared fields of interest. Thanks to a fantastically supportive group of parent educators on Facebook—you know who you are—for your generosity and encouragement. And last, a heartfelt thanks to Sarah Turner, whose editing expertise and friendship has been truly valued and appreciated.

A special acknowledgement goes to Fielding Graduate University's Institute of Social Innovation for supporting my work through it's post-doctoral fellowship program and for providing partial funding for my research.

Most importantly, without my family this book would not have been possible. My daughter, Sarah, helped me understand the importance of overcoming challenges and obstacles during adolescence. Observing how she developed the motivation to achieve her goals was one of the many seeds of my research. I especially thank my husband, Jay W. Mitchell, for his many years of encouragement, support, and patience. He not only allowed me the time and space to do my work, but has always encouraged me to follow my dreams. His dedication to my growth and development is an act of true love.

Reader Thank You & Invitation

Thank you for reading *Tomorrow's Change Makers*. There is only *one* reason I research and write on the topic of positive youth development—because I am passionate about educating and raising young people who are ready to thrive in the 21st century and beyond. I believe *all* of us make a difference in the lives of youth, and that we are collectively responsible for fostering a more caring, just, and sustainable society.

If you found this book insightful to your own work and/or relationships with young people, I would be honored by recommendations you make to friends and colleagues, including through social media. Reviews at Amazon, Goodreads, and other online bookstores make a huge impact on how books get noticed and shared. I am indebted to readers who take the time to write reviews, and for any feedback you might offer.

As my research continues on the *The Compass Advantage*™ (Chapter 6) and the variety of contexts where children gain core developmental competencies, I invite stories from adults and youth. In particular, I seek examples of how young people were specifically impacted by parents, teachers, and adult mentors in ways that helped them develop any of the eight core compass abilities. Teachers who are interested in assigning reflective student essays on these topics, please contact me. I always welcome anonymous student stories to include in my research and writing.

Please feel free to connect with me in any of the following ways:

- My blog for parents, teachers, and youth mentors at RootsOfAction.com (You can sign up for my eNewsletter and/or use the contact form there.)
- My professional website with contact form: MPriceMitchell.com
- Twitter: @DrPriceMitchell or @RootsOfAction
- Facebook: Facebook.com/RootsOfAction
- Pinterest: Pinterest.com/RootsOfAction

Again, thank you for your interest in youth civic engagement and for supporting today's young people. Together, we make a difference for all children and the society in which they grow and develop.

Warmly,

Marilyn Price-Mitchell, PhD

References

Akgun, S., & Ciarrochi, J. (2003). Learned resourcefulness moderates the relationship between academic stress and academic performance. *Educational Psychology*, 23(3), 287-294. doi: 10.1080/0144341032000060129

Albright, M. I., Weissberg, R. P., & Dusenbury, L. A. (2011). School-family partnership strategies to enhance children's social, emotional, and academic growth. Newton, MA: National Center for Mental Health Promotion and Youth Violence Prevention, Education Development Center, Inc.

Althof, W., & Berkowitz, M. W. (2006). Moral education and character education: Their relationship and roles in citizenship education. *Journal of Moral Education*, 35(4), 495-518. doi: 10.1080/03057240601012204

Anderman, E. M., & Murdock, T. B. (Eds.). (2011). *Psychology of academic cheating*. Academic Press.

Andolina, M. W., Jenkins, K., Zukin, C., & Keeter, S. (2003). Habits from home, lessons from school: Influences on youth civic engagement. *Political Science and Politics*, 36, 275-280. doi: 10.1017/S104909650300221X

Argyle, M. (2013). *Cooperation (Psychology Revivals): The basis of sociability*. Routledge.

Bandura, A. (1994). Self-efficacy. In V. S. Ramachaudran (Ed.), *Encyclopedia of Human Behavior* (Vol. 4, pp. 71-81). New York, NY: Academic Press.

Bandura, A. (2001). Social cognitive theory: An agentic perspective. *Annual Review of Psychology, 52*, 1–26.

Barber, B. R. (1992). *An aristocracy of everyone: The politics of education and the future of America.* New York, NY: Oxford University Press.

Benson, P. L. (1997). *All kids are our kids: What communities must do to raise caring and responsible children and adolescents.* San Francisco, CA: Jossey-Bass.

Berger, J. G. (2004). Dancing on the threshold of meaning: Recognizing and understanding the growing edge. *Journal of Transformative Education, 2*(4), 336–351. doi: 10.1177/1541344604267697

Berk, L. E. (2007). *Development through the lifespan* (4th ed.). New York, NY: Allyn & Bacon.

Berkowitz, M. W. (2000). Civics and moral education. In B. Moon, S. Brown, & M. Ben-Peretz (Eds.), *Routledge International Companion to Education* (pp. 897–909). New York, NY: Routledge.

Bertalanffy, L. (1956). General systems theory. In L. Bertalanffy & A. Rapoport (Eds.), General Systems: Yearbook of the Society for the Advancement of General Systems Theory (Vol. 1, pp. 1–10). Ann Arbor, MI: Society for General Systems Research.

Biswas-Diener, R., Kashdan, T.B. (2013). What happy people do differently. *Psychology Today,* July 2, 2013. Retrieved July 13 from https://www.psychologytoday.com/articles/201306/what-happy-people-do-differently

Blakemore, S. J., & Choudhury, S. (2006). Development of the adolescent brain: implications for executive function and social cognition. Journal of Child Psychology and Psychiatry, 47(3-4), 296–312.

Boyte, H. C. (1991). Community service and civic education. *Phi Delta Kappan, 72*(10), 765–767.

Boyte, H. C. (2005). Reframing democracy: Governance, civic agency, and politics. *Public Administration Review, 65*(5), 536-546. doi: 10.1111/ j.1540-6210.2005.00481.x

Brandtstädter, J., & Rothermund, K. (2002). The life-course dynamics of goal pursuit and goal adjustment: A two-process framework. *Developmental Review, 22*(1), 117-150. doi: 10.1006/drev.2001.0539

Brigham Young University. (2009, November 5). Benefit of a mentor: Disadvantaged teens twice as likely to attend college. *ScienceDaily.* Retrieved July 13, 2015 from www.sciencedaily.com/releases/2009/11/ 091104161837.htm

Carter S.S., Harris J., Porges S.W. (2009): Neural and evolutionary perspectives on empathy; in Decety J., Ickes W. (eds): *The Social Neuroscience of Empathy.* Cambridge, MIT Press, pp 169–182.

Centre for Addiction and Mental Health. (2013, January 15). Youth mentoring linked to many positive effects, new study shows. *ScienceDaily.* Retrieved July 13, 2015 from www.sciencedaily.com/releases/2013/01/ 130115143850.htm

Clandinin, D. J., & Connelly, F. M. (2000). *Narrative inquiry: Experience and story in qualitative research.* San Francisco, CA: Jossey-Bass.

Colby, A., & Damon, W. (1992). *Some do care.* New York, NY: Free Press.

Colby, A., & Sullivan, W. M. (2009, Winter). Strengthening the foundations of students' excellence, integrity, and social contribution. *Liberal Education,* pp. 22-29.

Coley, R. J., & Sum, A. (2012). *Fault Lines in Our Democracy: Civic Knowledge, Voting Behavior, and Civic Engagement in the United States.* Princeton, NJ: Educational Testing Service.

Cote, J. E., & Levine, C. G. (2002). *Identity formation, agency and culture.* Mahwah, NJ: Erlbaum.

Cozolino, L. (2013). *The social neuroscience of education: Optimizing attachment and learning in the classroom:* WW Norton & Company.

Creswell, J. W. (2003). *Research design: Qualitative, quantitative, and mixed methods approaches* (2nd ed.). Thousand Oaks, CA: Sage.

Csikszentmihalyi, M. (1997). *Finding flow: The psychology of engagement with everyday life* (1st ed.). New York, NY: Basic Books.

Csikszentmihalyi, M. (2014). Society, culture, and person: A systems view of creativity. *The Systems Model of Creativity* (pp. 47-61): Springer Netherlands.

Csikszentmihalyi, M., Rathunde, K., & Whalen, S. (1993). *Talented teenagers: The roots of success and failure.* Cambridge, UK: Cambridge University Press.

Dahl, R. E. (2004). Adolescent brain development: A period of vulnerabilities and opportunities. Keynote address. *Annals of the New York Academy of Sciences, 1021*(1), 1-22. doi: 10.1196/annals.1308.001

Damon, W. (2003). *Noble purpose: The joy of living a meaningful life.* Radnor, PA: Templeton Foundation.

Damon, W. (2004). What is positive youth development? *The ANNALS of the American Academy of Political and Social Science, 591*(1), 13-24. doi: 10.1177/0002716203260092

Damon, W. (2008). *The path to purpose: Helping our children find their calling in life.* New York, NY: Free Press.

Damon, W. (2011). *Failing liberty 101: How we are leaving young Americans unprepared for citizenship in a free society.* Palo Alto, CA: Hoover Institution Press.

Damon, W., Menon, J., & Bronk, K. C. (2003). The development of purpose during adolescence. *Applied Developmental Science, 7*(3), 119 – 128. doi: 10.1207/S1532480XADS0703_2

Davila, A., & Mora, M. T. (2007). *Do gender and ethnicity affect civic engagement and academic progress? Circle Working Paper 53.* College Park, MD: Center for Information and Research on Civic Learning and Engagement.

Deci, E. L., & Ryan, R. M. (1985). *Intrinsic motivation and self-determination in human behavior.* New York, NY: Plenum.

Deresiewicz, W. (2014). Excellent Sheep: *The Miseducation of the American Elite and the Way to a Meaningful Life.* NY: Free Press.

Dewey, J. (1916). *Democracy and education: An introduction to the philosophy of education.* New York, NY: MacMillan.

Dewey, J. (1933). *How we think.* Buffalo, NY: Prometheus Books.

Dewey, J. (1938). *Experience and education.* New York, NY: Kappa Delta Pi.

Diener, E. (2009). *New findings on happiness.* Paper presented at the First World Congress on Positive Psychology, Philadelphia, PA.

DuBois, D. L., Portillo, N., Rhodes, J. E., Silverthorn, N., & Valentine, J. C. (2011). How effective are mentoring programs for youth? A systematic assessment of the evidence. *Psychological Science in the Public Interest, 12*(2), 57-91.

Durlak, J. A., Weissberg, R. P., Dymnicki, A. B., Taylor, R. D., & Schellinger, K. B. (2011). The impact of enhancing students' social and emotional learning: A meta-analysis of school-based universal interventions. *Child development, 82*(1), 405-432.

Dweck, C. S. (2006). *Mindset: The new psychology of success.* New York, NY: Ballantine.

Eccles, J. S., & Gootman, J. A. (Eds.). (2002). *Community programs to promote youth development.* Washington, DC: National Academy Press.

Erikson, E. H. (1950). *Childhood and society.* New York, NY: Norton.

Erikson, E. H. (1958). *Identity and the life cycle.* New York, NY: W.W. Norton & Company.

Erikson, E. H. (1968). *Identity, youth, and crisis.* New York, NY: Norton.

Fagerberg, J. (2004). Innovation: A Guide to the Literature. In J. Fagerberg,

D. C. Mowery, & R. R. Nelson (Eds.), The Oxford Handbook of Innovations (pp. 1-26). Oxford, UK: Oxford University Press.

Fergus, S., & Zimmerman, M. A. (2005). Adolescent resilience: A framework for understanding healthy development in the face of risk. *Annual Review of Public Health, 26*(1), 399-419. doi: 10.1146/annurev.publhealth.26.021304.144357

Flanagan, C. A. (2003). Developmental roots of political engagement. *PS: Political Science & Politics, 36*(02), 257-261.

Flanagan, C. A., Gallay, L. S., Gill, S., Gallay, E., & Nti, N. (2005). What does democracy mean?: Correlates of adolescents' views. *Journal of Adolescent Research, 20*(2), 193-218. doi: 10.1177/0743558404273377

Foschi, R., & Lauriola, M. (2014). Does sociability predict civic involvement and political participation? *Journal of Personality and Social Psychology, 106*(2), 339.

Friedland, L. A., & Morimoto, S. (2005). *The changing lifeworld of young people: Risk, resume-padding, and civic engagement. Circle Working Paper 40.* College Park, MD: Center for Information & Research on Civic Learning & Engagement.

Friedman, L. J. (1999). *Identity's architect: A biography of Erik H. Erikson.* New York, NY: Scribner.

Gergen, K. J. (1994). Mind, text and society: Self-memory in social context. In U. Neisser, & R. Fivush (Eds.), *The remembering self: Construction and accuracy in the self-narrative* (pp. 78-104). Cambridge, UK: Cambridge University Press.

Gilligan, C. (1982). *In a different voice: Psychological theory and women's development.* Cambridge, MA: Harvard University Press.

Gonzales, D. (2007, January 16). A church's challenge: Holding on to its young. *New York Times.*

Goldstein, S., & Brooks, R. B. (2012). *Handbook of resilience in children*: Springer Science & Business Media.

Goodstein, L. (2006, October 6). Fearing the loss of teenagers, evangelicals turn up the fire. *New York Times*.

Greenleaf, R. K. (1977). *Servant leadership: A journey into the nature of legitimate power & greatness* (25th anniversary ed.). Mahwah, NJ: Paulist Press.

Gruber, Matthias J., Gelman, Bernard D., & Ranganath, C. (2014). States of curiosity modulate hippocampus-dependent learning via the dopaminergic circuit. *Neuron, 84*(2), 486-496. doi: 10.1016/j.neuron.2014.08.060

Hansen, D., Larson, R. W., & Dworkin, J. B. (2003). What adolescents learn in organized youth activities: A survey of self-reported developmental experiences. *Journal of Research on Adolescence, 13*(1), 25-55.

Hart, D., & Fegley, S. (1995). Prosocial behavior and caring in adolescence: Relations to self-understanding and social judgment. *Child Development, 66*(5), 1346-1359.

Hetheringon, M. J. (2008). Turned off or turned on? How polarization affects political engagement. In P. Nivola, & D. Brady (Eds.), *Red and blue nation? Consequences and correction of America's polarized politics* (Vol. 2). Washington, DC: Brookings Institute Press.

Howe, N., & Strauss, W. (2000). *Millennials rising: The next great generation*. New York, NY: Random House.

Huffington, A. (2014). Thrive: *The third metric to redefining success and creating a life of well-being, wisdom, and wonder*. NY: Harmony Books.

Jennings, M. K., & Niemi, R. M. (1981). *Generations and politics*. Princeton, NJ: Princeton University Press.

Jones, S. M., Bouffard, S. M., & Weissbourd, R. (2013). Educators' social and emotional skills vital to learning. *Phi Delta Kappan, 94*(8), 62-65.

Josselson, R., Lieblich, A., & McAdams, D. P. (Eds.). (2002). *Up close and personal: The teaching and learning of narrative research.* Washington, DC: American Psychological Association.

Kahne, J. E., & Sporte, S. E. (2008). Developing citizens: The impact of civic learning opportunities on students' commitment to civic participation. *American Educational Research Journal.* doi: 10.3102/0002831208316951

Kahne, J. E., & Westheimer, J. (2006). The limits of political efficacy: Educating citizens for a democratic society. *PS: Political Science & Politics, 39,* 289-296. doi: 10.1017/S1049096506060471

Kashdan, T. B., Sherman, R. A., Yarbro, J., & Funder, D. C. (2013). How are curious people viewed and how do they behave in social situations? From the perspectives of self, friends, parents, and unacquainted observers. *Journal of Personality, 81*(2), 142-154. doi: 10.1111/j.1467-6494.2012.00796.x

Kashdan, T.B., & Steger, M. (2007). Curiosity and pathways to well-being and meaning in life: Traits, states, and everyday behaviors. *Motivation and Emotion, 31*(3), 159-173. doi: 10.1007/s11031-007-9068-7

Kogan, Steven M., Brody, Gene H., & Chen, Yi-fu. Natural mentoring processes deter externalizing problems among rural African American emerging adults: A prospective analysis. *American Journal of Community Psychology,* 2011; DOI: 10.1007/s10464-011-9425-2

Kohlberg, L. (1981). *Essays on moral development: The philosophy of moral development* (Vol. 1). San Francisco, CA: Harper & Row.

Kohlberg, L. (1984). *Essays on moral development: The psychology of moral development* (Vol. 2). San Francisco, CA: Harper & Row.

Konrath, S.H., O'Brien, E.H., & Hsing, C. (2011). Changes in dispositional empathy in American college students over time: A meta-analysis. *Personality and Social Psychology Review,* 15, 180-198.

Kovan, J. T., & Dirkx, J. M. (2003). "Being called awake": The role of transformative learning in the lives of environmental activists. *Adult Education Quarterly, 53*(2), 99-118. doi: 10.1177/0741713602238906

Kroth, M., & Boverie, P. (2000). Life mission and adult learning. *Adult Education Quarterly, 50*(2), 134-149. doi: 10.1177/07417130022086955

Larson, R. W. (2000). Toward a psychology of positive youth development. *American Psychologist, 55*(1), 170-183. doi: 10.1037//0003-066X,55.1.170

Larson, R. W., & Hansen, D. (2005). The development of strategic thinking: Learning to impact human systems in a youth activism program. *Human Development, 48*, 327-349. doi: 10.1159/000088251

Larson, R. W., Hansen, D., & Walker, K. (2005). Everybody's gotta give: Development of initiative and teamwork within a youth program. In J. L. Mahoney, R. W. Larson, & J. S. Eccles (Eds.), *Organized activities as contexts of development* (pp. 159-183). Mahwah, NJ: Erlbaum.

Larson, R. W., & Kleiber, D. (1993). Daily experience of adolescents. In P. Tolan, & B. Cohler (Eds.), *Handbook of clinical research and practice with adolescents* (pp. 125-145). New York, NY: Wiley.

Larson, R. W., & Walker, K. (2005). Processes of positive development: Classic theories. In P. A. Witt, & L. L. Caldwell (Eds.), *Recreation and youth development*. State College, PA: Venture.

Larson, R. W., & Walker, K. (2010). Dilemmas of practice: Challenges to program quality encountered by youth program leaders. *American Journal of Community Psychology.*

Leinaweaver, Jeff. (2015) *Storytelling for Sustainability: Deepening the Case for Change.* Oxford, UK: Dō Sustainability.

Leone, C. M., & Richards, M. H. (1989). Classwork and homework in early adolescence: The ecology of achievement. *Journal of Youth and Adolescence, 18*, 531-548. doi: 10.1007/BF02139072

Lerner, R. M. (2007). *The good teen.* New York, NY: Random House.

Levine, P. (2007). *The future of democracy: Developing the next generation of American citizens.* Lebanon, NH: Tufts University Press.

Liang, B., Spencer, R., West, J., & Rappaport, N. (2013). Expanding the reach of youth mentoring: Partnering with youth for personal growth and social change. *Journal of Adolescence, 36*(2), 257-267.

Lieblich, A., Tuval-Mashiach, R., & Zilber, T. (1998). *Narrative research.* Thousand Oaks, CA: Sage.

Lopez, M. H., Levine, P., Both, D., Kiesa, A., Kirby, E., & Marcelo, K. (2006). *The 2006 civic and political health of the Nation: A detailed look at how youth participate in politics and communities.* College Park, MD: Center for Information and Research on Civic Learning and Engagement.

Lou, H. C. (2015), Self-awareness—an emerging field in neurobiology. Acta Paediatrica, 104: 121–122. doi: 10.1111/apa.12876

Luthar, S. S., Barkin, S. H., & Crossman, E. J. (2013). "I can, therefore I must": Fragility in the upper-middle classes. *Development and Psychopathology, 25*(25th Anniversary Special Issue 4pt2), 1529-1549. doi: doi:10.1017/S0954579413000758

Marcia, J. E. (1966). Development and validation of ego identity status. *Journal of Personality and Social Psychology, 3*(5), 551-558.

Marcia, J. E. (2004). Why Erikson? In K. R. Hoover (Ed.), *The future of identity: Centennial reflections on the legacy of Erik Erikson.* Lanham, MD: Lexington Books.

Marcia, J. E., Matteson, D. R., Oriofsky, J. L., Waterman, A. S., & Archer, S. L. (1993). *Ego identity: A handbook for psychosocial research.* New York, NY: Springer Verlag.

McLaughlin, M. W., Irby, M. A., & Langman, J. (1994). *Urban sanctuaries: Neighborhood organizations in the lives and futures of inner-city youth.* San Francisco, CA: Jossey-Bass.

Mezirow, J. (1991). *Transformative dimensions of adult learning.* San Francisco, CA: Jossey-Bass.

Morrell, A., & O'Connor, M. A. (2002). Introduction. In E. O. O'Sullivan,

A. Morrell, & M. A. O'Connor (Eds.), *Expanding the boundaries of trans-formative learning: Essays on theory and praxis* (pp. xv-xx). New York, NY: Palgrave.

Nakamura, J., & Csikszentmihalyi, M. (2014). The motivational sources of creativity as viewed from the paradigm of positive psychology *The Systems Model of Creativity* (pp. 195-206): Springer Netherlands.

Oatley, K. (1992). Integrative action of narrative. In D. J. Stein & J. E. Young (Eds.), *Cognitive Science and Clinical Disorders* (pp. 151-172). New York, NY: Academic Press.

Pajares, F., & Urdan, T. C. (2006). *Self-efficacy beliefs of adolescents*. Charlotte, NC: Information Age Publishing.

Palmer, Parker J. (2011). *Healing the heart of democracy: The courage to create a politics worthy of the human spirit*. San Francisco, CA: Jossey-Bass.

Pancer, S. M., Pratt, M., Hunsberger, B., & Alisat, S. (2007). Community and political involvement in adolescence: What distinguishes the activists from the uninvolved? *Journal of Community Psychology, 35*(6), 741-759. doi: 10.1002/jcop.20176

Patton, M. Q. (2002). *Qualitative research & evaluation methods* (3rd ed.). Thousand Oaks, CA: Sage.

Pea, R. (2004). The social and technological dimensions of scaffolding and related theoretical concepts for learning, education, and human activity. *Scaffolding: A Special Issue of the Journal of the Learning Sciences, 13*(3), 423-451.

Pinnegar, S., & Daynes, J. G. (2007). Locating narrative inquiry historically. In D. J. Clandinin (Ed.), *Handbook of narrative inquiry: Mapping a method-ology* (pp. 3-34). Thousand Oaks, CA: Sage.

Polkinghorne, D. E. (1988). *Narrative knowing and the human sciences*. Albany: State University of New York Press.

Price-Mitchell, M. (2010). *Civic learning at the edge: Transformative stories of highly engaged youth.* (Doctoral Dissertation), Fielding Graduate University, Santa Barbara, CA.

Putnam, R. D. (2000). *Bowling alone: The collapse and revival of American community.* New York, NY: Simon & Schuster.

Robson, C. (2002). *Real world research* (2nd ed.). Malden, MA: Blackwell.

Rutter, M., & Rutter, M. (1993). Developing minds. London: Penguin.

Sackett, P. R., & Walmsley, P. T. (2014). Which personality attributes are most important in the workplace? *Perspectives on Psychological Science, 9*(5), 538-551. doi: 10.1177/1745691614543972

Schneider, B. L., & Stevenson, D. (1999). *The ambitious generation: America's teenagers, motivated but directionless.* New Haven, CT: Yale University Press.

Schon, D. A. (1983). *The reflective practitioner: How professionals think in action.* New York, NY: Basic Books.

Sears, D. O. (1975). Political socialization. In D. O. Sears (Ed.), *Handbook of political science.* Reading, MA: Addison-Wesley.

Siegel, D. J. (2013). Brainstorm: The power and purpose of the teenage brain. New York, NY: Penguin.

Simha, A. (2014). Cheating in college—why students do it and what educators can do about It. *Academy of Management Learning & Education, 13*(1), 143-145. doi: 10.5465/amle.2014.0019

Steinberg, L. (2007). Risk taking in adolescence. *Current Directions in Psychological Science, 16*(2), 55-59.

Steinberg, L. (2010). A behavioral scientist looks at the science of adolescent brain development. *Brain and Cognition, 72*(1), 160-164.

Stevens-Long, J., & Commons, M. L. (1992). *Adult life: Developmental processes* (4th ed.). Mountain View, CA: Mayfield.

Taylor, E. W. (2007). An update of transformative learning theory: A critical review of the empirical research (1999-2005). *International Journal of Life-long Education, 26*(2), 173-191. doi: 10.1080/02601370701219475

Teske, N. (1997a). Beyond altruism: Identity-construction as moral motive in political explanation. *Political Psychology, 18*(1), 71-91.

Teske, N. (1997b). *Political activists in America: The identity construction model of political participation.* University Park: Pennsylvania State University Press.

Thacher, D. (2006). The normative case study. *American Journal of Sociology, 111*(6), 1631-1676. doi: 10.1086/499913

van Hoof, A. (1999). The identity status field re-reviewed: An update of unresolved and neglected issues with a view on some alternative approaches. *Developmental Review, 19,* 497-556. doi: 10.1006/drev.1999.0484

Veenman, M. V., & Spaans, M. A. (2005). Relation between intellectual and metacognitive skills: Age and task differences. *Learning and Individual Differences, 15*(2), 159-176.

Verba, S., Schlozman, K. L., & Brady, H. E. (1995). *Voice and equality: Civic voluntarism in American politics.* Cambridge, MA: Harvard University Press.

von Stumm, S., Hell, B., & Chamorro-Premuzic, T. (2011). The hungry mind: intellectual curiosity is the third pillar of academic performance. *Perspectives on Psychological Science, 6*(6), 574-588. doi: 10.1177/1745691611421204

Vygotsky, L. S. (1978). *Mind in society: The development of higher mental processes.* Cambridge, MA: Harvard University Press.

Weil, L. G., Fleming, S. M., Dumontheil, I., Kilford, E. J., Weil, R. S., Rees, G., Dolan, R., & Blakemore, S.-J. (2013). The development of metacognitive ability in adolescence. *Consciousness and Cognition, 22*(1), 264-271.

Weissbourd, R., & Jones, S. (2014). *The children we mean to raise: The real messages adults are sending about values.* Cambridge, MA: Harvard Graduate School of Education.

Westheimer, J., & Kahne, J. (2004). What kind of citizen? The politics of educating for democracy. *American Educational Research Journal, 41*(2), 237-269. doi: 10.3102/00028312041002237

Wood, D., Bruner, J., & Ross, G. (1976). The role of tutoring in problem-solving. *Journal of Child Psychology and Psychiatry and Allied Disciplines, 17*, 89-100.

Wuthnow, R. (1995). *Learning to care: Elementary kindness in an age of indifference.* Cary, NC: Oxford University Press.

Yates, M., & Youniss, J. (1996). A developmental perspective on community service in adolescence. *Social Development, 5*(1), 85-111. doi: 10.1111/j.1467-9507.1996.tb00073.x

Yohalem, N., & Wilson-Ahlstrom, A. (2007). *Measuring youth program quality: A guide to assessment tools.* Washington, DC: The Forum for Youth Investment, Impact Strategies.

Youniss, J. (2006). Forming a political-moral identity through service. In A. Siwka, M. Diedrich, & M. Hofer (Eds.), *Citizenship education* (pp. 183-192). Munster, Germany: Waxmann Verlag.

Youniss, J., McLellan, J. A., & Yates, M. (1997). What we know about engendering civic identity. *American Behavioral Scientist, 40*, 620-631. doi: 10.1177/0002764297040005008

Youniss, J., & Yates, M. (1996). Community service and political-moral identity in adolescents. *Journal of Research on Adolescence, 6*(3), 271-284. doi: 10.1111/0022-4537.791998079

Youniss, J., & Yates, M. (1997). *Community service and social responsibility in youth.* Chicago, IL: University of Chicago Press.

Youniss, J., & Yates, M. (1999). Youth service and moral-civic identity: A case for everyday morality. *Educational Psychology Review, 11*(4), 361-376. doi: 10.1023/A:1022009400250

Zaff, J. F., & Michelsen, E. (2002). *Encouraging civic engagement: How teens are (or are not) becoming responsible citizens* (pp. 1-6). Washington, DC: Child Trends.

Zimmerman, B. J. (2001). Theories of self-regulated learning and academic achievement: An overview and analysis. In B. J. Zimmerman, & D. H. Schunk (Eds.), *Self-regulated learning and academic achievement: Theoretical perspectives*. Mahwah, NJ: Erlbaum.

Zukin, C., Keeter, S., Andolina, M. W., Jenkins, K., & Carpini, M. X. D. (2006). *A new engagement? Political participation, civic life, and the changing American citizen*. Oxford, UK: Oxford University Press.

Index

INDEX

About the Author

Marilyn Price-Mitchell, PhD, is a developmental psychologist, researcher, writer, and speaker. A fellow at the Institute for Social Innovation at Fielding Graduate University, her research focuses on positive youth development—how young people become caring family members, innovative workers, ethical leaders, and engaged citizens in an increasingly complex society.

With extensive experience in the fields of human and organization development, leadership studies, complexity science, and education, Marilyn has consulted for diverse organizations, including schools, nonprofits, and Fortune 500 companies (See *MPriceMitchell.com).* She is a parent, stepparent, grandparent, and longtime community leader who has worked tirelessly to build partnerships between families, schools, and communities.

Marilyn writes a research-based blog for parents, educators, and youth mentors at *RootsOfAction.com;* authors a regular column for *Psychology Today;* and is a contributor to *Edutopia.* She lives in Bainbridge Island, Washington, with her husband Jay Mitchell.

CPSIA information can be obtained at www.ICGtesting.com
Printed in the USA
LVOW08s1724040216

473715LV00009B/124/P